I WAS A CUB SCOUT ONCE

I WAS A CUB SCOUT ONCE

A MEMOIR OF HEALING AND HOPE

DAVID JENSEN

BRAINSTORM WAREHOUSE, LLC

ISBN: 979-8-9956582-0-7

Library of Congress Control Number: 2026909253

Published by **Brainstorm Warehouse LLC** Boulder, Colorado

Printed in the United States of America

10 9 8 7 6 5 4 3 2 1

For my aunt, uncle, and cousins, who gave me safety, laughter, nourishment, and the first true taste of unconditional love.

For the countless friends who have always accepted me for me.

For my best friend, whose gentle soul and friendship shaped my life and whose memory continues to guide my dreams.

For my childhood dog, who offered comfort, loyalty, and love in the years I needed it most.

And for my therapist, who walked beside me as I reclaimed my voice, my truth, and my life.

This book exists as a thank you to each and every one of you.

Little ones, you never did anything wrong. You deserved love,
protection, and joy. I'm giving them to you now.

— DAVID JENSEN

DISCLAIMER

This memoir reflects my personal experiences, memories, and perspectives. I have written these events to the best of my recollection. Some names, identifying details, and locations have been changed to protect the privacy of individuals. Any resemblance to actual persons, living or deceased, is coincidental and unintentional.

This book contains descriptions of childhood sexual abuse, trauma, and related experiences. These sections may be triggering for some readers. Please take care of yourself while reading and seek support if needed.

This memoir is not intended to provide medical, psychological, therapeutic, or legal advice. I am not a mental health professional, and nothing in this book should be used as a substitute for professional care, counseling, or treatment. If you are struggling or in need of support, please reach out to a qualified professional or someone you trust.

The views expressed in this book are my own and do not represent any organization, institution, or group with which I have been affiliated.

This story is shared with the intention of truth-telling, healing, and offering hope to others who may be navigating their own journeys.

AUTHOR'S NOTE

This book is the story of my life as I remember it — the truths I carried for far too long in silence, the wounds I worked hard to understand, and the healing that continues to unfold. Some memories arrived clearly; others surfaced slowly over time, and working through them shaped the man I am today. I have written them with honesty, care, and respect for the younger parts of me who never had a voice.

I did not write this memoir to shock or to harm, but to tell the truth as I lived it. My hope is that these pages offer connection, understanding, or even a small sense of companionship to anyone who has ever felt alone in their childhood pain. If you find pieces of your own story reflected here, please move gently. Take breaks when you need to. Your well-being matters more than any chapter. This book is not meant to provide advice or answers. It is simply one person's journey through trauma, healing, and the long road back to self-love and hope. I share it with gratitude for the people who helped me survive, the communities that held me, and the inner voice that kept whispering to keep going.

Thank you for reading my story. Thank you for witnessing it. And thank you for walking these pages with me. — David Jensen

NOTE ON MEMORY

Trauma does not preserve memory in straight lines. Some scenes remain sharp; others break apart, blur, or wait years before returning. On my healing journey, I've learned much about how early childhood trauma shapes recall. What follows is my best account of what I lived through, including memories that resurfaced long after the events themselves. Even when details are partial, the emotional truth and the reality of their impact remain faithful to my experience.

Some names and identifying details have been changed or omitted to protect privacy.

CONTENTS

PART I

CHILDHOOD

1

EARLY CHILDHOOD

When I think about the highlights of my childhood, a few memories come to mind. There was the child I appeared to be, and the one buried deep inside.

One of the first memories I had—before the sexual abuse memories surfaced—was visiting the fire department on a preschool field trip. It's a short memory, but I remember the big fire truck sitting in the driveway at the station.

As I write this, I wonder if I held on to that memory because it symbolized safety and strength. I didn't feel either of those as a boy. I had too many hidden secrets, never to be shared.

Safety was what I longed for from trusted adults. Internal strength didn't exist in any form inside me. That field trip showed me something different, and my younger self held on to that day and the gift it provided.

I participated in a handful of sports when I was young. I played soccer as a small boy and later football. I was the center on my football team. I was a chunky kid during that time.

I loved candy—my drug of choice. Lucky Charms cereal was my favorite: pure sugar and comfort. Candy was the numbing agent I needed to suppress what churned under the surface. I was trying to bury something I didn't yet understand.

I have one significant memory from a soccer game. During the game, I was accidentally tripped by a player on the opposing team. After the game, I approached the kid, made an accusatory comment, and forcefully shoved him. He tripped over his own foot and fell to the ground. My coach witnessed this, came over, and said, "If you ever do that again, I will bench you for the remainder of the season." No one bothered to ask why I was so angry, and I didn't have the words to explain it. Looking back, I see how much repressed anger that boy was carrying. I was that child, and it was not who I wanted to be.

I joined the swim team when I was nine years old. I loved swimming and felt an extreme sense of freedom in the water, especially deep underwater. There was something oddly comforting about being in that space.

I really liked my swim coach. He was this hippy dude who drove a VW Bus. I thought he was very cool. I used to spend summer days at the pool with my swim team friends.

A huge highlight of my first year in swimming was winning the "most improved" award. Awards were given out at the summer banquet, but we had to visit my father's parents—my grandparents—and I missed the banquet. I had no say in the matter, and I'm still saddened that I didn't get to attend. I wanted to be the boy who could say, "Mom, Dad, I really want to go to the swim banquet," but I didn't have the tools.

But the place where I felt most like myself wasn't on a field or in a pool—it was in Kansas.

One of the biggest highlights of my childhood was visiting my cousins and aunt and uncle in Kansas during the summers. Most of the time, my father didn't come with us, and I was quite fine with that.

It's a very small town. There are over 6,000 residents, and as a kid I thought they all knew each other. It felt like a community—and one I liked.

We hung out at the pool, took drives around town, played bingo at the VFW, went to the fair when it came to town, rode the small train at the park, and had picnics.

I noticed that my body changed in that environment. It relaxed. I felt less tense. I was able to be more present. It felt safer there. This was the boy I wanted to be all the time.

The environment, the community, and being around my aunt and uncle provided the nurturing I was missing. I couldn't articulate it then, but it was a bubble of complete and unconditional love.

When it was time to go back to Colorado, I never wanted to leave Kansas. During the drive home, I would go away—shut down. I had to be that boy again, the one who sank into a state of dissociation.

It is terribly painful to think about that poor child inside and what his body was doing to protect me.

I performed magic shows for relatives when I was a kid. Every Christmas for many years, I asked Santa for The TV Magic Kit. There were several kits, each with some pretty cool tricks.

I put on magic shows at family gatherings, and my cousin recently reminded me that I made her sell popcorn during the performance. That memory makes me smile.

I've wondered why I had such a passion for magic as a child. I'm not exactly sure. I know I would have liked to take my magic wand and make everything better for that young boy, but my normal was my normal.

I was involved with other organizations as a child. We attended Catholic church, and one of my brothers and I were altar boys.

I was also part of the Y Indian Guides when I was seven. It was supposed to be a father-son bonding experience, sponsored by the local YMCA. My name in the group was Running Deer, and my father's was Walking Deer.

We took a trip to a YMCA camp in the Colorado mountains with other boys and their fathers. We stayed in a dorm building for the weekend. I know we went swimming, but I remember nothing else from that trip.

I attended what was called an open living school from second to sixth grade. It was only four blocks from our house. It was a new concept where there were only a few classrooms, and the rest of the school was open—somewhat like a loft space—with partitions partially dividing the classes.

When I was in third and fourth grade, ages nine and ten, I became involved in scouting. I was a Cub Scout, and my mother was the Den Mother. My father, as I remember, was a volunteer—no official title, but he said he was a volunteer. He loved feeling important and I never knew why.

Until the abuse memories returned, the only memories I had of scouting were building my pinewood derby car in our basement with my father and the pack meetings in our home's basement. My neighbor friend Luke came to one scout meeting and never wanted to come back. I never knew why. For years, those were the only memories I allowed myself to have.

These early memories were the surface of a much deeper story—one I wouldn't uncover until my twenties.

2

—————

BLANK SPACES

I am 62 years old, and over the decades of working to heal from childhood sexual abuse, I have come to realize that whenever there are huge time periods in my life that I cannot remember, it's usually a clue that there may be something I need to look back on with curiosity.

I've read a few nonfiction books where people write about their early childhoods, and it seems like they remember everything. I've always been amazed that someone could recall so much from those early years. This certainly wasn't me.

Big holes of missing time during childhood often equal trauma. That is the pattern I've come to understand as I heal and reflect on those tender years. I mentioned in the last chapter that my earliest memory was the visit to a fire department in preschool. I was four years old.

My next specific memory before the sexual abuse memories surfaced was my fifth birthday. It's a short blip, but a very special day. I got a puppy for my birthday. We went to pick him up, and I remember he was in a cage you could lean over to pet the puppies. He was *puppying* around with his brothers and sisters.

I immediately picked him because he was the smallest—the runt of the litter. I sensed he needed some extra love and care.

When we got home, I ran into the backyard through the garage and sat down on the edge of our cement deck. He ran out after me, plopped off the deck onto the grass, twirled around with his tail wagging, and then ran over and jumped into my lap. I felt alive with joy.

I remember my mother saying, "What a dandy dog."

I named him *Dandy* that day. I still have that memory. I loved Dandy and learned the meaning of unconditional love from him.

There are two memories from kindergarten when I was five. One is nap time. We had mats that we got out and took naps on. That's all I remember, but it's a specific memory.

The second one has much more detail. It was one particular day when we made butter in the classroom with a real butter churn. Afterward, we ate it on saltine crackers. It tasted so yummy and smooth. I still remember the taste.

As for why I remember that one specific day, I'm not entirely sure —other than it was a very happy and joyful blip of time and fun to create something together with my classmates. Creating still gives me great pleasure.

Then came first grade, and with it a few days that stand out with clarity.

At age six, I remember being in school. Our grade met in a single classroom building at the end of our block. We got to have a treat one day a week, and that week it was orange juice. We were having it at the end of the school day. Each of us was assigned a certain day to dismiss the class, and this day was mine.

As I was dismissing the class, one of my female classmates vomited all over her desk. It freaked me out, and I said in rapid succession, "Rows 1, 2, 3, 4, 5 dismissed!"

I got the stomach flu a few days later. I was lying on the couch in our home one night, watching something on television. My mom was sitting behind me on the love seat. I started feeling bad and began to groan.

My mother jumped up from the couch, picked me up, and put her hand over my mouth as I vomited all over myself and down the hallway. In that moment, it felt more about keeping the carpet clean than nurturing her sick child. That memory is emblazoned in my mind.

Second grade, age seven: I remember looking at the list of teachers posted outside a window at the new open living school I attended, trying to see who my homeroom teacher would be.

Third grade, age eight: I do not remember much.

Fourth grade, age nine: I remember very little before the abuse memories. This would have been my first year as a Cub Scout. I remember really liking a class with one of my teachers. She was the science teacher, wore glasses like me, and was really cool. We took a field trip to a planetarium.

One random swimming memory: a winter night at the Foothills Recreation Center indoor pool. After practice, I was in the locker room with the other swimmers and my dad. I was getting dressed, wearing my Speedo swimsuit—black with dark blue stripes. I put on my t-shirt, then my shirt, then a sweater, then my winter jacket. Only after all of that did I take off my Speedo and put on my underwear and pants.

I wanted to hide my body—especially my genitals and backside—because I felt ashamed and unconsciously wanted to protect myself.

I was a scout at ages nine and ten. I couldn't tell you if it was two complete years or one year and part of another. Other than what I mentioned in the first chapter about scouting, I couldn't remember anything else from that time.

There are other memories from those younger years, but not many. All along the way, there were major gaps and missing time. Those blank spaces weren't my memory failing me—they were acts of survival.

I left home at eighteen to attend college.

I've thought a lot about what I've learned about memory over the past year—especially how highly emotionally charged memories are more deeply imprinted in our brains.

Many of the memories I wrote about in this chapter had a high degree of emotion attached to them—the challenging ones as well as the extremely pleasant ones. Because of that, I seem to remember more of those specific details.

These early memories were the fragments that remained while the rest stayed buried for decades.

3

MY NORMAL

I grew up in a house on the corner of a street in Applewood, Colorado. We were on the east side of Table Mesa Mountain. We had an always-groomed hedge separating the street and sidewalk from our home. The lawn was green and always mowed and, in the winter, the snow was shoveled by eight in the morning.

I was fed well and had clean clothes to wear. It looked like a sense of normal, but the real "normal" was unpredictability.

My father was an alcoholic, and there were many nights when he would come home extremely drunk. There were alcohol-fueled fights between my mother and father, and those disruptions often led us to leave the house in the middle of the night. We would end up staying at neighbors' homes down the street or at a hotel. This happened repeatedly throughout my childhood. It was frightening, disruptive, and wildly unpredictable. Despite all the chaos, the grass stayed mowed and green and perfect.

Being raised Catholic, I was conditioned to always tell the truth and obey the laws of the church, including the Ten Commandments.

During that same night, I remembered my father in the locker room after swim practice, dressing in safe layers. Something happened that tested my truth-telling.

We had driven my fellow swim team member and neighbor, Jen, and her brother to practice. As we drove home, Jen asked, "Have either of your parents ever been in jail?" I answered truthfully and honestly, "Yes." My answer was followed by an evil look from my father.

There had been an earlier incident when my mother had to call the police after my father came home drunk, and he was hauled off to jail.

We dropped off Jen and her brother. Silence filled the car as my father drove us home.

When we walked into the house, my father said, "Your mother should have been the one in jail that night." Then he beat me and sent me to my room. I was also grounded. Moments like that shaped how I understood my father—while confusing how I understood myself.

I told the truth, and the lesson I learned that night was never to tell certain parts of the truth. If you did, it would bring suffering, isolation, and pain. I was never given the rule book on which truths to tell and which ones not to tell.

This made me doubt not only myself and what I was taught by the church, but also what the acceptable level of truth was in a home.

If my father ever talked to me, it was on his terms, and that meant it was in the bathroom while he took a dump on the toilet. There was nothing meaningful about those moments. What was memorable was the nasty smell and my discomfort.

There was a lot of tension in my childhood home, and it played out in my body. My normal was to have at least three headaches per week. I didn't sleep well and had nightmares consistently. I had horrible stomach pains multiple times per week. The pains felt like someone was sticking pins deep into my stomach.

I thought this was what all kids lived with, and it became the normal. My normal. My conditioning was to never speak or complain about anything, because it would expose me to even more pain and suffering.

There was abuse in my household growing up, and coupled with what happened to me in scouting, the damage only compounded. I was programmed to eventually never speak much truth at all, so I stuck it on a shelf. This is how I learned to survive.

And although I didn't know it at the time, dissociation was becoming one of my normals. I had a hard time paying attention at school.

I was highly creative and used to write strange, dark stories. Many of them would have signaled the school staff to call Child Protective Services today. They were extremely dark and revealing.

I was also an overly clumsy child, and this was obvious during sports and other activities. I tripped a lot.

I couldn't relax when I learned how to ski and would lock my legs going down the hill. I wasn't in my body because it wasn't safe to be there—and that became another version of normal.

I had very few friends and spent much of my time with my dog or alone in my room, or spacing out watching television.

One pattern that played out multiple times in my life was the inability to stand up for myself. I was in a fight in elementary school and completely froze in front of the boy I was supposed to fight. He started punching me and kept going, and I never moved. I stood there frozen until the janitor came outside and intervened.

My normal was to take abuse and not fight back. I feel so much compassion for the young boy who had to normalize so many experiences that never should have been.

This was the unhealthy soil given to me—the version of normal that I carried into the rest of my life.

4

HEROES

Heroes who were there during my childhood were more than people I looked up to — they were lifesavers, although I didn't know it at the time. My aunt, uncle, and cousins in Kansas, my fifth-grade social studies teacher, and my swim coach and swim team friends all played that role.

My mother, my middle brother, and I took many trips to Kansas during my childhood summers. I always wanted to stay with my cousins and my aunt and uncle. I felt at home in their house because I could relax, be a kid, and feel safe in my body.

I couldn't have identified it then, but now I know I felt present to life there; my shoulders relaxed, my stomach relaxed, and I enjoyed being in the moment.

We would go to the swimming pool, watch movies on cable television, visit the zoo, have picnics, go to the small movie theater, frequent Dairy Queen, go to parks, and stop by the local Rexall Drug Store that even had a soda fountain.

All of this was heaven to my body, soul, and spirit. It gave my highly alert nervous system a much-needed break from the hypervigilance it defaulted to when I was back in Colorado.

My aunt and uncle loved me unconditionally and allowed me to be the child I was meant to be. They are my heroes, and I am forever grateful to them. My uncle passed away a few years ago, and before he died, he said to me, "Maybe we should have adopted you, Dave." I smiled as a tear filled my eye and responded, "I agree."

My cousins were heroes as well because we got along so well and enjoyed each other's company. Of course, we had little spats, but they were short-lived.

My one cousin and I still laugh about a rebellious moment at the Rexall Drug Store when we were kids. She reminded me of what the owner said before I was kicked out: "You belong in a pig trough." I had forgotten that comment — and whatever I did to bring it on. I see it now as an absolute challenge to an authority figure, one I knew wouldn't physically harm me. A big clue to something else going on in my life.

My aunt and uncle scolded us at times, but it was handled in a healthy way and life moved on. They never shamed us. This was a testament to how they parented — with unconditional love. They believed in letting you accept the consequences of your decisions, with the opportunity to correct your mistakes.

Back in Colorado, another hero showed up in a different setting — the pool.

I swam on the Aviation Club Swim Team from age nine until fifteen. We had the same swim coach the entire time. His name was Mark Henderson, and I remember him as this huge, broad-chested, hippy-like guy. He pushed all of us to be the very best we could be, and he didn't let up.

I used to swim backstroke and long-distance freestyle. My worst stroke was butterfly. During swim meets, Mark would put us in the events we were best at — and in the one we were most challenged by. I hated it, but I did it anyway. For me, that meant swimming the 100 Butterfly. I remember one meet where I was the absolute last kid in the pool. Mark walked along the deck beside me, cheering me on in full coach fashion: "Come on Dave, you can do it!" And although I was last, I finished. He will never know the mark he made on me growing up. He pushed me beyond my self-perceived — and unknown wounded — limits.

We used to have a huge July 4th celebration and barbecue at the pool. They would throw a watermelon into the water covered in Crisco, and whoever got it out won the watermelon. And every year, whoever won shared it with the other swimmers anyway, so it didn't really matter who got it out — everyone won.

It seemed like Mark was at the pool all day long. I remember helping make swim ribbons with one of my friends on the team, and we thought it was so cool. Being of service to others while being involved in a childhood passion was the lesson.

I think Mark sensed that I was the kid who needed additional support, and he didn't do it by favoring or babying me. He did it by showing me that safe adults exist — real role models. He pushed all of us to do our best.

Mark was a true hero during the same time I was in scouting. Several of my swim friends were heroes as well, and I was able to spend time with many of them.

One of my swim friends, Dell, had a swimming pool at his house — a real cement, in-ground pool. I loved going there. Growing up in Colorado, it was rare for anyone to have a pool. I felt safe enough at Dell's to be the kid I longed to be, even if only for a short time. His parents and brother were safe, loving people to be around. I learned that there are environments where adults provide structure and opportunities to grow — without harm.

Mr. Bennett, my fifth-grade teacher, was another hero. He drove a VW Bug, had a mustache, and I really liked him. He encouraged me, supported me, and accepted me. I had a racing mind from living a life where my nervous system was always on alert.

I remember one assignment in his social studies class that I didn't do very well on. He allowed me to do additional work on another topic to bring up my grade — something more creative. I loved the make-up assignment because I could exercise my creativity. I remember using colored construction paper, cutting out pictures from magazines, and gluing them onto the pages. Then I wrote with different markers to provide the story and facts about the country I featured. He liked it, and it improved my grade.

We also went on a field trip one day, and Mr. Bennett was going to drive his Bug. I wanted to ride with him. I asked my mother if I could, and she became very upset because she was also driving kids and wanted me to ride with her. I didn't want to ride with her. She must have caved, because I ended up riding with Mr. Bennett. He was another safe adult in a position of power — a hero in my life — and he saw me. I learned from him that there are always choices in life.

Sexual abuse teaches the opposite.

There were other heroes along my childhood journey — many were teachers — and I am grateful to every one of them. Having safe adult role models gave me an unrecognized strength to survive what I was dissociating from at the time. The things that the infinite wisdom of my body, mind, and spirit put in a compartment, never to be dealt with as a child.

These heroes kept me alive, and the support they provided became the places where my nervous system learned some semblance of safety, even if I didn't know it.

5

DREAMS

Reflecting on my childhood dreams is bittersweet. I think a lot about who I might have become if the sexual abuse had never happened — how many of those childhood dreams might have become reality.

The truth is that the abuse did happen, and those dreams became clouded by the need to survive.

Materialism has faded over the years, and the grief for a lost childhood — and the dreams that disappeared with those dark times — has been replaced by a desire for rich life experiences, a sense of belonging, love, autonomy, and the ability to fully live in the present.

I felt like I belonged on the swim team because there was guidance, support, camaraderie, and healthy competition, all driven by my passion for being in the water.

I felt like I belonged when I was spending time with my aunt and uncle and with my cousins in Kansas — the feeling of the humidity, the sound of cicadas at night.

I felt like I belonged in art class in elementary school. The class fed my creativity, and it was an unknown lifesaver at the time. I liked painting and drawing, and even enjoyed making the familiar clay ashtray that never actually got used. Joking aside, there was something therapeutic about working with clay. It was tactile and grounding and allowed me to express something I didn't yet have words for.

I felt like I belonged when participating in school plays and having the opportunity to be another character, even briefly — a character free of abuse.

Belonging was what I needed outside of the abuse. I still participate in many of these activities today and continue to seek out other safe arenas to belong. It is key to my ongoing healing.

Alongside belonging, I also had dreams of who I wanted to become.

One of the many occupations on my list of potential careers as a small child was veterinarian. I have always loved animals. I had my dog growing up, as well as a cat, a bird, some fish and gerbils.

My most favorite pet was my dog, Dandy. We had ten years together until that dream was shattered when my father shot and killed him.

Dandy brought me refuge from the dysfunction at home. He was joy wrapped in fur — the living symbol of complete and unconditional love. He showed me loyalty and affection without expecting anything in return during many troubling years.

I longed to be loved with no strings attached by my immediate family members and the adults in my life. Unfortunately, that longing was overpowered by being sexually abused by the very people I wanted love from. The unconditional want and need became conditional under those in positions of power.

I struggle less today to decipher whether another's love is conditional or unconditional. As I continue healing, I attract a higher quality of people in all areas of life. I still have work to do, but there has been immense healing.

I think autonomy is one of the greatest gifts we can give a child. Autonomy — "the ability to be self-governing" — must be nurtured over time. I longed for it as a child. But without many key, trusting adults to role-model, guide, and encourage autonomy, my ability to self-govern was lacking. I longed for that guidance from my parents and from the leaders in scouting, but instead I received the opposite — coercion, dependence, control, manipulation, and shame.

I did receive pieces of what I needed from others, and for that I am grateful. I continue to work on healing from the damage caused by being controlled by adults who should have offered me more positive, growth-filled opportunities. To be more independent earlier on. To test being out in the world under their safe guidance. To grow and learn and make mistakes on the road to becoming more independent — without punishment. To be encouraged to be safely different and embrace my uniqueness while developing my interests and talents.

Having the ability to fully experience the present — to embrace the joy of the moment and to be in my body, experiencing the world through the five senses: sight, hearing, smell, taste, and touch — was, and still is, a dream. I wanted this, and when I felt safe as a kid, I experienced glimpses of that joy.

As a child who suffered horrible sexual abuse, I learned to want to be anywhere but in the present moment. I survived by going away — dissociating — and not being here now. This saved my life, although I longed and dreamed for something else.

Feeling disconnected from one's own body is not living, and it played out in my clumsiness and struggles with physical tasks — skiing being one example.

Sexual abuse has created lifelong challenges around intimacy — especially sexual intimacy.

Being comforted with healthy touch was something I longed for as a child and so often did not receive. And when I did receive touch from those who abused me, it was anything but safe. It created deep confusion about what safe touch even meant at such a young and tender age.

When I look back at my dreams as a child, I didn't dream of owning an airplane, having a powerful career, or traveling the world. I dreamed of having the things every child should be given by the adults entrusted with their care — all without manipulation or harm.

I longed for belonging, unconditional love, opportunities to learn and experience true autonomy, nurturing, safety, and the ability to live fully in the present moment and explore my world.

All of these should be protectively provided by those in power to all children.

In many ways, I am still reclaiming these dreams today.

PART II

RED FLAGS

6

HIDDEN WOUNDS

Red flags littered my younger life. They were everywhere — nothing overly dramatic, but small blips of time. During those blips, there was humiliation and internal pain that played out repeatedly. I didn't know the cause, but something was terribly wrong. I never would have noticed it then. I couldn't. I had no insight.

There was a day in fourth grade when I was ten years old. This was during my scouting years.

Someone in art class had taken my pencil when the teacher momentarily left the room. I knew who took it. I wanted my pencil back — it was all I had to sketch with at the time.

I was terrified to confront the student, even over something so small. When the teacher returned, I raised my hand. My face was red. I remember my upper body shaking and feeling overwhelmed with anxiety. The teacher called on me: "David, what is it?"

It took every ounce of energy to stand up for myself and expose the identity of the person who had taken my pencil. I struggled to get the words and his name out. There were beads of sweat on my forehead. I don't remember what I said, but I remember the fear. The shame. It was horrible to feel those things — and this was only about a single pencil.

Earlier in this book, I mentioned a fight in elementary school where I completely froze until the janitor intervened. In junior high school, there was another freezing incident.

An older classmate had driven to school, which was forbidden and illegal because the driving age in Colorado was sixteen. I had witnessed Alex Rivera driving a van to school.

How I ended up in the vice principal's office telling on Alex, I'm not exactly sure. I told the truth about what I had seen and who had driven the van parked in the school lot.

A few days later, as I was walking home from school, the same van pulled up next to me. The side door slid open, and out jumped Alex Rivera. He rushed over and punched me in the nose.

I remember the pain and the blood that immediately rushed out and dripped onto my shirt. Tears filled my eyes and I cried. Alex said something threatening, got back in the van, and they drove off. I collected myself as best I could, blood still gushing from my nose and all over my shirt.

I was about three-quarters of a mile from home. I took my shirt off, stripping down to my t-shirt so no one would see the blood.

I arrived home, ran inside, and went straight downstairs to my room. I wanted to clean up so no one would know what had happened.

No one in my family ever found out, and I never said a thing. I was afraid I would get in trouble for not standing up for myself. My father had told me years before, "I'll kick your ass if I ever catch you running from a fight."

At fifteen, I had a beef with someone on my swim team. I don't remember what it was about, but there was going to be a fight over it. We agreed the fight would take place on a certain day at a certain time at the far end of the parking lot at the swimming club. I remember the trees there and how secluded that part of the lot felt.

He was waiting for me. As I approached, I saw him pick up a long piece of wood — I believe it was a 2x4.

I walked closer. He cocked his arms back, holding the weapon, and swung it at me like a baseball bat. The wood hit me on the right side of my body. I think I blacked out right before I was hit because I don't remember any pain.

My body dissociating. My body taking over and protecting me when I couldn't do it for myself.

There was another individual I grew up with — Jason Brewer — and he was a bully. He turned on me during my junior high years.

I played soccer with Jason for a short time. He had the ability to recruit others to join in when he bullied people, and I joined him in bullying others at times.

I was an awkward kid and would miss kicking the soccer ball because I wasn't connected to my body. I was extremely dissociated and had no idea. Imagine a kid running up to a soccer ball, trying to kick it, and completely missing — that was me.

Jason nicknamed me "Animal." I think it was because he knew I would never fight back. I didn't know how. When he called me *Animal*, it enraged me.

Our temporary assistant coach chewed tobacco, and one day he spit his chew out and it hit my leg. I honestly don't know if it was an accident or on purpose. The slimy tobacco spit dripped down my leg. The coach started laughing and said, "Sorry, Animal."

Everyone around laughed. I felt an overload of shame. I didn't say anything and died a little more inside that day.

I chose to go to a different high school from Jason to avoid him. I would run into him at parties from time to time. I wanted to kick his ass because he had been such an absolute fucker to me.

Jason tormented me for a long time in junior high, and I never got the chance to beat the shit out of him. I wanted to — and I had no knowledge of how to fight.

During all these situations, I never once fought back. Not one hit. Ever. I just took the abuse. Why couldn't this kid fight back? What did that boy never learn? Were the hidden wounds running my life?

The freeze responses were a direct result of what I learned as a small boy when I was being sexually abused: freeze. Disappear inside. Float away. This response was ingrained into every cell of my being. I was taught to be submissive and never fight back. I was also trained early on to never tell a living soul what was happening. Telling the truth was a death sentence.

The life tools to stand up for myself were never offered. I didn't have the courage to tell a trusted adult what was going on and ask for advice because the immediate adults in my daily life were also abusing me.

I wasn't in touch with the memories. And so, I was left to fend for myself by freezing, avoiding, or hiding in plain sight as best I could. If I had had someone I felt safe enough to talk to about these things, they would have noticed a pattern.

Freezing and dissociating were my protectors and default settings — decades before I knew why.

7

———————

ACTING OUT

As I look back at my childhood, I see that some of my questionable behavior was really about wanting to be seen and wanting to belong. It was just coming out sideways.

I wasn't conscious at the time of what I was yearning for or the strange ways I was reaching out. It was all acting out. Bullying, stealing, provoking people — these were the only ways I knew to feel like I belonged, or to have some power, or to feel anything at all during the time I was being abused.

I mentioned Jason Brewer bullying me previously, and the strange thing is that he was a friend years before he turned on me. When I was in elementary school and hung out with Jason, there was an incident we both instigated one Saturday afternoon. I was a bully that day too.

We decided to visit our elementary school playground. It was huge, with all the unsafe playground equipment that used to exist — and lots of it. One of the most popular structures was a red metal tower, probably a 10–12 foot climb to the top.

You could climb up on metal bars, and once you reached the top, there was a sectioned-off platform where you could sit or stand. A rubber railing wrapped around the top to keep people from falling.

Three sisters from our school were on top of the tower having a picnic lunch that day. Jason and I climbed up, terrorized the three of them, and stole their lunch.

This made me feel powerful over someone else for a change. I don't remember many details, other than one or more of the girls crying after we took their food. Jason and I climbed down with their lunches. They were still screaming and crying as we walked away.

It was a rush to feel powerful — like I finally belonged while doing an evil deed. Unhealthy belonging, but belonging nonetheless. I feel bad about what I did that day.

Something else took place in elementary school that was ongoing. There was a kid named Evan Carter, and he used to eat his boogers.

Looking back, I did too — but in private. I used to do it in my bedroom, along with wiping them on the wall next to my bed. Yep.

Jason and a few other bullies used to make fun of Evan, and one day I joined in as the other boys egged me on. It was another rush of power, and it seeped through my dissociated normal state of being.

I got off on it, and I would make fun of Evan repeatedly after that day. He was an awkward kid (much like me), but I had found my sick tribe with Jason and the other bullies. I thought they had my back, which created a sense of safety. The bullying coincided with the years I participated in scouting and beyond.

I had lunch with a childhood friend, Derek Hartley, several years ago. We shared stories about our childhoods and remembered some of our classmates from elementary school.

Derek mentioned that he had run into Evan years earlier, and Evan told him that I had ruined his life. That was hard to hear, and in that moment, I felt a huge sense of regret for participating in picking on Evan all those years ago.

That wasn't the only time I sought power in strange ways.

I was visiting my cousins in Kansas about a year later, and my aunt took us to the zoo. We stopped for lunch at a fast-food restaurant in town.

I went to the bathroom, and as I was coming out, a guy — probably in his twenties — was standing right outside the door. I decided to stand in front of him and block the doorway. I wouldn't move. When he tried to pass, I stepped into his path and made a rude comment.

He was with a woman.

My cousins Elise and Terry were right next to me. My aunt was outside in the car.

The man didn't do anything, and I kept egging him on, trying to aggravate him. I was testing someone else's boundaries, seeing how far I could push them, and I felt invincible doing it.

This feeling of power was addictive. I know he could have easily kicked my ass, but he didn't do a thing.

My cousin Terry said, "Mom's waiting for us." I pushed past the guy, giving him a nasty look.

He just stood there. I had succeeded in provoking an adult and "winning," at least in my mind. It felt good to turn the tables on an adult.

I used to steal during the time I was a scout. I had a friend in elementary school, Buddy Whitman. He was a badass kid, and I liked hanging out with him. I felt powerful being around Buddy.

One day, we were in a 7-11 type store. He said, "David, steal me some Bubble Yum."

The best gum ever.

I said, "Sure." I wanted to maintain his friendship.

Buddy went outside, and I stayed behind and stole a pack of gum. I met him afterward and gave him the gum behind the store. I belonged. I felt powerful. Adrenaline surged through me. I did this to finally take up space in the world.

During another childhood heist, I wasn't so lucky.

I was in the Safeway grocery store near our home with my mother and father. I was walking around by myself and decided to steal a multi-pack of gum. I walked down the candy aisle, thinking no one else was there, and took the gum off the shelf. I quickly shoved the packets down my pants.

Suddenly, a voice behind me said, "Where's the gum you just stole?" I turned around, and it was an adult employee.

I said, "What gum?"

He responded, "The gum you just put in your pants."

Instant fear and shame overcame me.

My parents could have turned down that aisle at any moment.

I pulled the gum out of my pants pocket and handed it to him, my face now cherry red.

The employee said, "Get out of here, and I never want to see you in this store again."

I was surprised.

A part of me may have wanted to be caught. Maybe, unconsciously, I thought jail would be safer than home or scouting.

I left the store and waited outside for my parents. They came out and we went home. I didn't go back into that store for years, and my mom and dad never found out.

After the Safeway experiment, I thought I could get away with anything — even if I was caught in the act.

One late afternoon, I was in my mother's closet and decided to steal money from her purse. She caught me right as I was dumping some change into my hand. "David, what are you doing?"

We were supposed to go shopping at the mall that night, and she said we wouldn't be going.

She also told me I would have to tell my father what I had done. I told him while he was taking his evening shit in the bathroom — and he did nothing. He would have beaten the crap out of me on any other day, but this time he didn't.

Writing about acting out and stealing repeatedly, I think about the "Why?" Why was this kid doing all of this? Yes, the theme of wanting to belong, to feel something — even fear, adrenaline, or power — was part of it. It was something beyond numbness.

Underneath it all, I was calling out for help.

The bullying was my attempt to reclaim the power that unhealthy adults were stealing from me.

Acting out was one of the only ways I could feel anything through the numbness.

8
____

DISSOCIATION AND ISOLATION

Dissociation and isolation were two painful survival behaviors that engulfed my childhood.

Dissociation saved my life during the abuse, but it robbed me of being present in my own life. Isolation from others felt safer, but it also kept me from experiencing connection, joy, and belonging.

I have spent decades working to undo both survival tactics, and while I've made much progress, they still ripple in and out of my life.

Imagine going through life so protected in body that you are not in your own body. Always wondering when the next sexual abuse episode could happen. Being so on guard in mind and body that your nervous system takes control, living daily with hypervigilance.

Dissociation is the worst feeling when you are present with it. It's like being pulled away from your body even though you don't want to go. Pulled so far away that you are approaching death. Dark. Distant. Alone.

I became a human doing, not a human being. Rarely in my body, I developed an extremely high pain tolerance as a kid.

I was abused at home and in scouting, and my nervous system never had the opportunity to relax. It was continuously on high alert, and my energy was directed at saving my life even after the threat was gone. I learned to be on high alert day and night — like a machine with no heart and no spirit. A surviving machine living outside of its core being.

One spring day when I was ten years old, my middle brother and I were walking in a field about half a mile from our house.

There was a broken fence, and my brother jumped over it. As I hopped over, my leg got caught on something. I didn't feel anything. I just climbed over the fence and scurried past my brother.

A short time later, he yelled from behind me, "David, your leg is bleeding." I looked down and didn't see anything.

He pointed again. "Look — the back of your leg."

I looked down and behind my lower right leg. It was dripping blood.

I had caught the lower part of my leg on some downed barbed wire, and I didn't feel a thing.

I have a scar to this day on the back of my right leg from the accident. Another example of how I lived outside of my body.

Dissociation also played out when it came to deeply experiencing emotions. Having my life threatened by the adult abusers if I ever told anyone sends a deep message to your emotional being: do not feel.

During the sexual abuse, I would black out so I wouldn't feel the terror, anger, and rage.

I have struggled my entire life to be completely emotionally present. My body still has a backlog of unprocessed feelings.

I have often shared with friends and therapists how many unshed tears I carry from the sexual abuse I suffered as a child.

My current therapist is always pleased when I let out more of the deep anger and rage stored from what happened to me. Those two feelings were absolutely and completely forbidden by the abusers. Expressing either would have gotten me killed or severely hurt.

The feelings had to freeze and go away — dissociate themselves from me — to save my life. It wasn't okay to have any feelings.

This included the positive ones. Good feelings were complicated.

I am much better today at expressing emotions, but the pleasant ones — joy, happiness, laughter, contentment — are still challenging to fully surrender to. One deeply ingrained, painful thought I experience when I feel positive emotions is that they are going to abruptly end with more abuse. So why feel them?

Spending more time in the good is something I continuously work on, and it's scary at times. The messaging I received around all feelings was to simply not have them. Emotions drew attention — and attention could expose the secret.

Dissociation fed the isolation, and I was happier and safer being alone in my room or sitting outside with my dog, watching the other kids in the neighborhood play. Keeping my distance kept me safe in my mind.

I remember many years ago trying to have a conversation about the abuse with my mother. She loved to shut me down whenever I tried to talk about it.

She would block and shift to another hurtful comment: "You were such a loner as a boy."

The comment enraged me.

This was at a time in my life when I was becoming more aware of my childhood. I had no idea how triggering it would land.

I retorted, "I'm not a loner."

I didn't stay long visiting her that day.

Those who abuse us want to keep us small, even years later in adulthood.

A child should be taught how to socialize and feel safe expressing themselves around others — not discounted, shamed, and retraumatized.

The abuse taught me that adults are not safe, especially those who are supposed to be trusted and in positions of power.

I have a photo album filled with pictures of me during my youth. I was looking at the pictures years ago.

As I looked at myself in many of them, my eyes seemed glazed over. I thought, "That kid is not in his body."

I wasn't.

The photos were eerie to look at. Most of them were a very disturbing view.

Pictures of children should be filled with life, joy, and happy experiences.

Dissociation and isolation were the major ways I moved through the world until the memories returned.

9

———

FEARS

Fear was the primary emotion programmed into every cell of my being. It was the main architecture of my early years, and that relentless programming created a blueprint for my later ones.

I feared my parents when I was a child. My father was abusive — mentally, physically, and sexually.

My mother was abusive and a narcissist. Corporal punishment was practiced extensively in our home.

I remember one time when my middle brother and I were playing downstairs. We had made clay bowling pins and a clay bowling ball.

My brother went to roll the clay ball, and it stuck briefly to his right palm before flying out of his hand and into a glass shelving unit behind the bar, shattering the glass.

My mother came downstairs and asked who had broken it. I don't know who spoke up, but the truth came out: it had been an accident, and it was my brother who broke the glass.

My mother, filled with rage, retrieved the wooden yardstick and said that since both of us were playing, both of us would be punished.

She brutally beat the yardstick against my brother's rear end until it broke. As I witnessed his beating, fear filled my body, knowing I was next.

I was bent over and beaten, frozen in fear, just taking it.

I was beaten for playing a game — and for an accident. As I write this, I am filled with anger because it *was* an accident. We were honest about what had happened.

That day taught me once again that telling the truth was deserving of punishment. Accidents are intentional. And one should always and forever fear their parents. These were the messages my body absorbed.

Another memory: an early Sunday morning. My father opened the front door to get the newspaper and made a nasty remark to summon us all to the doorway.

The outside trees, bushes, porch, and lamp post had all been extensively toilet-papered.

My brother knew it was probably some of his friends.

I remember standing there with my mother, brother, and father, looking out at the mess. My father made another nasty comment.

I chimed in and said, "Those pricks!" — a word my father used all the time.

He grabbed me from behind. I tensed and froze in fear.

He wore pointed-toe dress shoes.

He cocked back his right leg and delivered a powerful kick to my ass. It was extremely painful, and I burst into tears.

Being beaten this intensely made me feel worthless as a child.

Two over-the-top reactions by both parents — one for an accident, the other for using a word my father used constantly. These beatings had lasting effects because they happened at such a young age.

I wonder today what was going on inside either of them to unleash so brutally on their children. Those episodes imprinted themselves on my developing body, mind, and spirit, feeding my fear of authority figures then and later in life.

Fear, in whatever form it showed up, compounded itself

throughout my childhood. Having limited to virtually no safe adult to talk to only made it worse. I stuffed as much of it away as I could.

Those memories didn't stay in childhood — they shaped how I maneuvered through the world.

I avoided conflict with authority figures for much of my life, afraid of being lashed out at. I am in a much better place with fear today, understanding that I was groomed and programmed to be fearful of adults in and out of scouting.

Fear of dying — to an irrational degree — has been with me for most of my life. I never knew why for a very long time. This fear always intensified when more sexual abuse memories surfaced.

I now know that my life was threatened repeatedly by many of the sexual abusers.

When your life is threatened and you are sworn to secrecy about horrific abuse being acted out upon you, it creates lifelong fears. Looking at them, talking about them, writing about them brings them to the surface — and eventually helps you understand them more.

Over the last five years, as I've worked through old and new scouting abuse memories during the settlement process, I've had more memories of being told I would be killed if I ever spoke about the abuse.

That fear intensifies until it subsides, and there is no knowing how long it will take. As a kid, this was all operating under the surface, buried — but fear is strong, and there is no way to completely stuff it down.

I have tried to write a memoir about the sexual abuse perpetrated upon me for decades and always stopped due to the fear of going public and being killed for doing so. That type of fear has been paralyzing at times.

When it comes to living joyfully and experiencing success, all the old fear programming is triggered and surfaces. The fear backlog becomes jumbled into my current life and spills over into many areas. I think this is because it triggers being seen and heard — living life on a larger scale.

This plays out today in subtle and not-so-subtle ways. I am continuously working to separate what happened as a child from what is happening now.

Today, I continue to work on owning my talents and dreams and pursuing them. I continue to work on accepting the expertise I've developed in my chosen work life.

I continue to work on the fear — and on living bigger in the world.

When the fears surface, I try to acknowledge them, trace them back to their birth, sit with those wounds, let them grieve, and then move forward into more living.

It is very hard work. Work no one should ever have to do.

My childhood fears became the engine that drove my life. Today, I can slow down and remind myself that was the past — and try to choose courage over fear.

10

SELF-ESTEEM

I applied to graduate schools around the country in my fifties with a focus on writing. It was something I had wanted to do decades earlier, but after many years of healing, I finally felt ready to pursue this dream.

I asked a few individuals to write letters of recommendation, and one person I highly respect — someone who knows me and my craft well — wrote in his letter to the admissions committee, "I wish David had more confidence in himself."

I have made a lot of progress when it comes to self-esteem and self-confidence. And with all the healing work, I am still shaped by the childhood sexual abuse. Foundational childhood wounding.

As a young boy, I enjoyed swimming and artistic endeavors. When I swam, I felt held and comforted by the water and was able to tune out most of the outside world.

Creative writing, making things in art class, and acting in plays allowed me to escape into a creative realm much safer than being completely present. I had passion for these things, and they kept my self-esteem and low confidence from plummeting into the abyss.

Awkwardness and lack of confidence showed up in other sports I was involved in — football, soccer, skiing. This was due to my inability to fully inhabit my body. Fear was playing out unconsciously through freezing and dissociating. It made it extremely difficult for all my body parts to work in unison. Less so when I swam, because the water supported me.

I remember hating skiing because I could not unlock my knees going down the hill. My hips and legs locked. Unlike many skiers who use the flexibility in their hips and legs to absorb the shock of the mountain, my limbs were constantly in shock — unconsciously bracing for the next abusive event.

My body remembered what my mind couldn't yet face.

Continuing to explore, mourn, and reparent the child I was remains some of my most important ongoing work. I was never able to express the deep levels of grief as they were happening during the abuse. I was too frightened, and all my energy went into the physical mechanics of surviving. All available energy rushed to my core.

Abuse takes away one's self-esteem and confidence little by little. It has a cumulative effect. It tears down and destroys some of the most essential elements of childhood growth.

I have put much thought into wondering how I ever lived through one abuse incident, much less multiple.

In scouting alone, there were somewhere between seventeen and twenty-two separate sexual abuse acts. This all happened in less than two years. Each one horrific in its own way.

I was perpetrated by an adult volunteer in New Mexico and a scoutmaster in Colorado, repeatedly — both using me to exert their power and carry out their sick, illegal sexual acts.

And then afterward, in my most vulnerable state, being told I was a horrible person and not to be believed. It eats at one's soul and core. And with all of it, I did not die.

Over the course of my healing, I have been able to get in touch with something deep inside me.

I call it the Spark.

It is the piece of me I cannot completely explain. A point deep inside — a place of absolute strength. It lives in the depths of my spirit. And it can never be destroyed. It is that inner glow that is life, unique to each of us.

I am not a religious person, but I consider myself spiritual and part of something bigger than me — something universal.

It is something all good, and my spark is a part of it. I am grateful for that part of me.

I feel the spark inside is what allows me to continue revisiting, unpacking, and healing from the core damage done by cowards much older than me who tried to destroy every ounce of my being.

Truth-telling, speaking, and writing this book restore the confidence taken from me and assist in rebuilding my self-esteem. As cliché as it sounds, there is power in telling the truth. And healing.

I was told by the abusers that I was crazy after being abused and that "nothing happened." It *did* happen — to me and to countless others in scouting.

Awareness is a gift — even when it doesn't feel like one.

We are unable to work on any of our struggles until we become aware of them.

As I have become more aware of the scouting abuse, the more I feel the need to tell my story. In doing so, I no longer carry it alone.

And as I share my story with the world, another person may see a part of themselves in it — and that may ignite the spark inside them to seek help, to start or continue their healing journey.

11

BODY STUFF

I had no clue as a child that my body was holding so much sexual abuse trauma. It offered me clues in the form of headaches, stomach aches, spacing out, right ear issues, throat problems, numbness, posture issues, neck pain, and others. Many of these issues I still carry today, sometimes to a lesser degree and sometimes stronger.

I had at least three headaches a week as a child. It was my normal. My father used to tell me I had bad hay fever, and I believed him. I was given Excedrin to deal with the headaches and reminded that hay fever causes headaches.

The headaches were intensely painful. I don't remember ever telling a doctor about them. When a physical symptom is your normal, you learn not to question it.

I thought that was how all bodies worked. I know now that the amount of stress placed on my body during the sexual abuse had to take a toll.

I remember crouching outside the school by the gymnasium during recess, curled in the fetal position, holding my stomach in horrible pain.

I had many stomach aches throughout my childhood, and this carried into adulthood.

Decades of tests and upper endoscopies eventually revealed Barrett's esophagus, a precancerous condition. I had multiple procedures to treat it and must be consistently monitored, which requires a tube being put down my throat under sedation.

I have had trouble swallowing since early childhood. I've been diagnosed with a hiatal hernia, irritable bowel syndrome (IBS), and diverticulosis.

My digestive system freezes up during times of stress, during sleep, and when I have sexual abuse memories. These GI issues have been some of the most frustrating lifelong challenges I've had to deal with. I've exercised most of my life, and the GI symptoms never matched my lifestyle.

I started doing my own research and found that my symptoms match medical research on childhood sexual abuse. There is a long-term connection between childhood sexual abuse and the development of gastrointestinal issues later in life — and I am proof of that fact.

There is so much research out there, and for someone who has experienced these issues for decades, it is something no person should ever have to deal with when it is directly linked to being abused as a small boy. It is my lifelong reminder of the past abuse and the toll it takes on the body.

The early childhood signs were signals — my body calling out for help from the very areas it was being abused.

My body was holding the trauma in multiple ways.

I've mentioned dissociation many times as a protective mechanism, and when I have memories today or am triggered by something that reminds me of the abuse, it comes on and I feel myself trying to leave my body.

It shows up as spacing out, becoming clumsy, losing periods of time, feeling lightheaded, and having a feeling of wanting to die.

This is my system feeling under threat, activating my nervous system to take all available energy and bring it to the core. My body trained itself to do this, and it activates even when there is no threat.

I am better at recognizing it now, but it's a bitch to manage sometimes.

When it comes on, I have to sit down, concentrate on my breathing, slow everything down, and comfort myself. When it comes on full force, I need to completely check out by taking a nap so my body can try to balance out and calm down.

My posture suffered as a child. I wasn't aware of it at the time, but I loved being in the fetal position when I napped or slept. I was told to sit up straight a lot because I slouched. My default posture as a kid was collapse.

I've visited chiropractors throughout my life. I still struggle to sit up straight. My neck sits forward, my spine is curved, and doctors have told me I have kyphosis — a curvature of the upper back. This is a direct after-effect of the sexual abuse.

My body grew around the abuse as a form of protection. The fetal position is a great position for a baby, but not for an adult.

There is a specific area in my lower abdomen — just left of my belly button, down into the left lower quadrant. I've had horrible cramps there since childhood. After I started getting in touch with the abuse, several massage therapists pointed out how much tighter my left abdominal area was compared to my right.

The more work I've done, the more I've noticed that some memories are stored in that area. I call it the epicenter of my sexual abuse. For some reason, a great deal of the trauma froze in that specific spot.

So much of my trauma was stored in my body. All these physical ailments were how my body dealt with the abuse as best it knew how. My body did this so I wouldn't be overwhelmed — because the full force of the abuse would have been too much for me to survive. Trauma is tough on anyone, but it is life-threatening to a child during the act.

Healing is lifelong work, and judging when to push, when to relax, and when to stop is something I've had to learn the hard way.

I was working with a therapist during a time when I was having many body sensations and memories, often during sessions. I just wanted to push through and get all the trauma out once and for all.

One day, it was happening again. I was shaking, trembling, feeling everything. I wanted it all out for the last time.

My therapist interrupted the process after it had gone on for a long time. He was forceful with his words: "David, you need to slow down — you're retraumatizing yourself."

I learned that day about the need for more patience with myself on the healing journey. And this is always countered by the extreme desire and frustration to get all the trauma out.

My body had always remembered — and was reminding me about the past abuse long before I had the knowledge to understand what it was saying.

PART III

THE ABUSE MEMORIES

12

SURFACING

My first sexual abuse memory surfaced after my father died, when I was nearly twenty-seven. Until that moment, I would have sworn I had never been sexually abused.

The day the first memory arrived, it was one involving my father sexually abusing me at a very young age. It threw my life into chaos until I sought help. Being sexually abused by multiple family members has had an unfolding of its own.

I have worked with well over ten different therapists and explored many different modalities.

My experience is that sexual abuse memories surface in waves. Riding those waves is challenging in every way — emotionally, physically, mentally, and spiritually.

I have learned more about childhood trauma and sexual abuse than I ever thought existed, nor ever cared to know, quite frankly.

When I am unable to remember extensive periods of time from my childhood, it's usually a big clue. This pattern often signals that there was abuse — sexual or otherwise.

I was taught and programmed to deny and stuff the truth way down below. My body, mind, and spirit aligned and worked together to completely dissociate. All for one, one for all. This crushed my spirit.

My father sexually abused me repeatedly as a child. I have had many of those memories over many years. My father was involved in scouting as a volunteer. I do not remember his specific position.

My mother was involved with many of my childhood sports, activities, and clubs. She was also the Den Mother for my Cub Scout troop.

I began sensing that there was deeper abuse involving my mother about ten years ago. Years before, when the memories first began, she would say to me in an angry tone, "When are you going to be over all of this?"

I see now that my memories were creating alarm bells inside her. My mother's denial and secrets about what was happening in our home ran deep, and hearing that statement multiple times was extremely hurtful.

Within the last decade, I had a horrible sexual abuse memory involving my mother when I was a young boy. She forced me to perform oral sex on her. After the act, she said, "If you ever tell anyone, it will kill mommy."

For weeks after that memory surfaced, I was sick to my stomach.

And then there was scouting — another place where my memory went dark.

Both of my parents were involved with the scouting organization and its activities.

I was a Cub Scout in 1972 and 1973. I remember working on my pinewood derby car with my father in the basement. There was inappropriate kissing between my father and me.

There was a Cub Scout meeting in our basement one day, and my neighborhood friend, Luke Galloway, came to visit. He never wanted to come back, and I do not remember why. I still don't.

My mother never wanted me to be friends with Luke, and I didn't understand why.

I tried to remember the names of the other scouts in my pack during the settlement process and had not been able to recall any of them earlier in the process.

I do remember that we had the larger pack meetings in a Methodist church a few blocks away. Other than that, I remembered little to nothing else. This gap only signaled to my gut that something horrible must have happened. That feeling continued to grow stronger.

Shortly after I learned about the BSA settlement and the call to submit an initial Proof of Claim, I started to wonder if my father and mother had abused other children. I will never know.

Even now, as I write this, part of me dissociates.

It is still hard to grasp that a parent could sexually abuse their own child.

At the time I filed my initial claim, I had many sexual abuse memories and estimated that I had been sexually abused hundreds of times as a child. I probably had twenty or so specific memories at that time.

The recent release of the Epstein files parallels much of my own experience.

There was cover-up in my family. No one wanted to talk about the sexual abuse, and everyone denied — and still denies — it.

The reality is that in my family, every single person who sexually abused me took it to their grave and was never held accountable.

Neither of the scouting abusers was ever held accountable.

I have a commitment to telling the truth, and writing and talking about my story is part of that truth-telling.

Memories never returned all at once — they returned in fragments, and each one reshaped my understanding of my childhood.

13

THE FIRST BIG SCOUTING MEMORY

My memory of the pinewood derby car incident with my father, coupled with the memory of my friend never wanting to attend another Cub Scout meeting at our house, were hints of more to come.

I've often heard that healing unfolds like an onion — layer after layer until there are few to no more.

I have had sexual abuse memories come to me in many ways. My first surfaced at a twelve-step meeting. Many have surfaced during therapy sessions. I had one while I was out running.

I have had multiple abuse memories during massages. I have had them during acupuncture treatments. Memories have surfaced while sitting and listening to music. I have had memories show up in the form of nightmares in the middle of the night.

The BSA settlement process has been a long, intense, and thorough journey. I have experienced the onion peeling away along this long road, and more scouting abuse memories have presented themselves in the last five years.

I have participated in individual therapy for many years and continue to do so regularly. I have also seen the same therapist for many years and feel completely safe with this individual.

I had been working extensively on the required materials for the BSA settlement and had a therapy session the next day.

I will never forget that day.

It was beautiful outside; the sun was shining. I remember how good I felt before the session.

There had been some reprieve from months of abuse memories involving my oldest brother.

I was working very hard to practice maximum self-care while integrating many of those memories. I was feeling lighter in my daily life.

I lay down on the couch in my therapist's office, focused on my breathing, and began to relax.

Soft, comforting music played in the background. I felt safe and peaceful — something rare, but something I work on embracing more.

I started to feel a sense of dread and fear, and then suddenly, a small fragment of an individual's last name came to me. It came out of nowhere.

I kept sounding it out. It was like it was unfolding in my mind. It was the strangest thing.

As I continued to speak the last name out loud, it became clearer. I kept repeating it, over and over. It was a very specific last name — one I wasn't familiar with before.

Then the first name entered my mind. A simple name. I put the first and last name together. I repeated the full name. I repeated both names over and over.

And then the picture arrived.

I saw an older adult — dark hair, shirt off, smooth chest, a beefy guy. He was much older than me.

The snapshot in my mind was very clear. He was standing in front of a lake.

As the memory continued, I knew it was a Boy Scout camp. A camp in New Mexico. I didn't get the name of the camp, but I knew it was in New Mexico. It was a fishing trip with older scouts and younger scouts like me — a Cub Scout.

This man was a volunteer, either an assistant or a much older scout. I saw a fishing pole in front of the lake. A deeper feeling of dread washed over me.

The picture shifted: I was in a tent on my hands and knees, and he was forcing a long, thin cylindrical object into my anus. It was not his penis.

Immediately, everything went blank. I dissociated.

The next part of the memory came, and I told my therapist that there had been a big cover-up regarding what happened. No specifics — just a deep knowing. Nothing more.

I began to sob.

I cried and cried. I couldn't stop.

My therapist comforted me. I felt like I was going crazy. The memory hit me like a ton of bricks, out of nowhere.

I remember feeling like I was having a psychotic split. I was terrified. I did not want to lose my mind.

I sobbed more — deep, guttural sobs for what felt like forever. The tears eventually subsided. The crazy feeling passed.

I was alive.

This was one of the scariest abuse memories I had ever experienced.

I don't know how I got to the camp. I don't remember seeing if others were around. I don't know how long I was at the camp. I do know it was warm out.

I do not know if I went to the hospital.

I do not know how I got home.

I do not know the age of the individual, other than that he was much older than me.

I left my therapist's office that day in a zombie-like state. I was in shock, but also relieved — as if something long buried had finally been freed. As horrible as I felt, I felt lighter.

As the memory became clearer since that day, I would estimate his age between seventeen and twenty-five years old, or older. He was an adult — that I do know — and I was nine or ten years old.

I do my own fact-checking when I have very specific memories.

I was fascinated that a name had been burned so deeply into my memory. I looked online to see where most people with that specific last name live in the United States.

The results came up: New Mexico.

I did more research and discovered that the more emotionally charged the abuse, the more specific the details get encoded into the brain.

The brain encodes the highest threat, and other details that are lesser emotionally charged are not encoded — things like the specific camp, how I got there, how I got back to Colorado.

I am still working through the impact of having this memory. There are more tears yet to be shed. There is ongoing integration work to do.

I will never fully understand why I was the target at that scouting camp in New Mexico. I will never know what happened to the man who abused me. I will never know if he abused other kids. I do not know if he is alive or dead.

What I do know is that the incident scarred me for life, and I am grateful I lived through that day. I am grateful the memory has been freed from my psyche.

That day in my therapist's office was when I realized the scouting memories were deeper and darker than I had ever imagined.

14

MORE ABUSE MEMORIES

The New Mexico memory opened a locked door and allowed more sexual abuse memories to surface — both inside and outside of scouting.

I had more memories of my oldest brother sexually abusing me anally and orally. Those memories eventually calmed over a number of months, and then the first church basement memory emerged involving my scoutmaster in Colorado.

Our larger scouting meetings took place in the Methodist church only blocks from the house I grew up in.

I am in the basement of the church, standing in front of the scoutmaster. He is sitting in a folding metal chair. I do not see his face. It's blurry in my memory, as if there is a film or haze over it.

Something is protecting me from seeing exactly what is going on. I do know it is the scoutmaster because I say his name.

He is making me perform oral sex on him.

My face buried in his crotch.

I disappear. I dissociate.

And then it is over.

After the abuse, the scoutmaster says, "Nothing happened."

"This didn't happen."

"You're a Cub Scout. I am the scoutmaster. You are crazy if you think anyone would believe you."

"Put your cap on and go upstairs and join the other scouts."

I walk toward the basement steps to the right. As I get close to the stairs, the scoutmaster says, "Scouts Honor."

It is a command.

I feel a deep sense of disgust.

I turn around and hold up my right hand — two fingers raised, thumb across the others — the Cub Scout sign at the time.

I turn away, and that part of the memory stops.

And then the scene shifts.

The next thing I remember, I'm in the upstairs church area. Tables are set up in the room, and I am sitting at one in the middle. I am on one side, with other scouts beside me and across from me.

I hear the voices of adults around me, but I do not see them.

I see myself sitting in the middle of this table full of other scouts. I don't see their faces, and I don't know who they are.

I am frozen, full of shame and disgust.

I feel completely alone in a room full of other scouts and adults.

I cannot describe how horrible the feeling is — the worst had just happened, and I cannot tell another soul. I sit there motionless and dissociated.

The next thing I remember is hearing the scoutmaster's voice. I don't see him, but I know it is him. He is talking loudly to other adults, loud enough for me to hear.

"Crazy kids, crazy kids, Bob."

He says "crazy kids" many times.

I am confused because Bob is my father's name. Why is he saying this to my father?

I burst into tears in my therapist's office.

Long, deep sobbing.

As the memory starts to subside, I tell my therapist how sad that poor little boy must have felt — how alone he felt afterward.

I continue to cry, and my therapist asks, "How can you comfort that little boy now?"

He hands me a pillow, and I hug it and cry and cry and cry.

I say to the pillow, "I am so sorry that that happened to you."

I feel crazy again, coming out of the memory.

Another memory surfacing out of nowhere.

More memories followed that day. All were more of the same.

All involved the scoutmaster making me perform oral sex on him in the basement of the church. During one memory, my focus was locked on how hairy and musky and stinky his crotch smelled.

He kept saying, "Suck that B— D—!"

He was very forceful that day, his hands around my head.

Afterward, he said, "Nothing happened."

Then another memory.

Again in the church basement.

This time he is overly forceful, much like the one before, and after it is done, the familiar recurring phrase: "Nothing happened."

I believed everything adults told me. I was told to tell the truth, and I did.

I was an altar boy. I was told not to lie, and when I did, I was punished.

So being told that something so brutal — something that kept happening — "didn't happen" was too much for my underdeveloped brain to handle, much less process. So I filed it away in the "never to be dealt with" file.

I was realizing now that the oral abuse in Colorado with the scoutmaster was not a single incident, but a pattern.

15

FLOODING

I experienced a flooding of memories over the next few months — one after another, relentlessly.

I had somewhere between twelve and seventeen additional memories involving the same scoutmaster, and all but one involved sexual abuse on me. All took place in the church basement, isolated from the other scouts, alone with the same monster. Some of the memories were beyond brutal.

Many began with physical sensations: horrible pain in the back of my neck, tightness in my throat, and extreme sensitivity when drinking or eating — symptoms I still experience today.

There was a continued theme around what the scoutmaster said during the abuse — degrading, violent language meant to humiliate and dominate.

"Suck that B--- D---!"

Several of the memories surfaced during therapy. One day, in the middle of a particularly intense memory, I opened my eyes, looked at my therapist, and said, "Why is it that all perpetrators think they have suck bi— di---?" We shared a brief laugh, and that small moment of levity helped me get through the memory.

I have a friend in California who was also horribly abused as a child. We talk often. Sometimes we find ourselves laughing about the absurdity and cruelty of what was done to us. In those moments, we know healing has taken root. The laughter lightens the brutality. It reminds us that the abusers have no power over us anymore. The damage was done — and we are working to heal.

But the memories involving the scoutmaster kept coming.

More dialogue surfaced — more threats, more degradation, more attempts to control me through fear.

"Suck that B--- D---! You *faggoty* little Cub Scout."

One phrase was new: "If you tell anyone, I will kill you." No wonder I buried everything so deeply.

One day, I was looking at the only photo I have from scouting — an 8x10 picture of a play I was in. I'm on the right side wearing my scout cap. In front of me is another scout.

As I studied the picture, I realized who the other boy was: Nathan Ellis, who lived across the street from me.

A short time later, after recognizing Nathan in the photo, the worst scouting memory surfaced.

I was in my therapist's office, relaxed, focusing on my breathing. My eyes were closed. And then, out of nowhere, the memory arrived.

I saw Nathan. I didn't see his face, but I knew it was him. His name came to me instantly.

He was positioned in front of me, completely naked. I had the overwhelming sense that he might be unconscious — or worse.

I see his feet and legs and butt directly in front of me. He is frozen.

A familiar voice came from behind me, over my left shoulder. The scoutmaster. He was issuing commands — forceful, repeated, escalating.

"Stick it in him, David."

"Stick the pencil in his butt."

"Stick the pencil in him."

He just kept repeating these commands over and over. I don't know how many times.

Nathan isn't moving.

I blacked out.

The next thing I remember is the scoutmaster's voice saying, "David, now you are just like me."

Then the scene shifted.

I was standing at the front door of Nathan's house across the street. Nathan's mother was at the door, saying something to me, though I couldn't see her face: "David, Nathan is not allowed to play with you."

The memory shifted again — foggy, disjointed. A male adult voice said, "He moved because of you."

I didn't see who said it. I only heard it.

The memory faded, and I began to convulse and sob. I cried and cried and cried. My therapist comforted me.

Working through that specific memory is an ongoing process.

Being forced to participate in such a sadistic act involving my childhood friend, fellow scout, and neighbor has carried lifelong impact.

I was a child — forced, manipulated, terrorized — and then told I was "just like him."

I have struggled with sexual intimacy my entire life. During penetration, I cannot maintain an erection because I feel like I am hurting the other person. Now I know where that programming was born.

When I began writing this memoir, I questioned whether to include this memory. Should I? I kept asking myself.

The answer was always yes.

I wanted to provide the absolute truth about what happened to me as a child in scouting. It was brutal. It was wrong. People need to see the devastation it causes.

Over 80,000 initial Proof of Claims were filed in the BSA settlement. Many survivors never completed the process. I know I cannot be the only one who suffered this level of brutality.

My abuse happened in the basement of a church while children and adults were upstairs.

Where were my protectors?

This one memory showed me the full extent of the scoutmaster's cruelty — and the depth of the damage I still carry today.

16

THE BSA SETTLEMENT PROCESS

I first became aware of the BSA settlement process early in 2020. I learned that to be part of the settlement, I would need to submit a Proof of Claim by November 16, 2020. I had no clue what a Proof of Claim even was. I didn't understand the scope of the bankruptcy, the structure of the settlement, or really anything about the process.

I sat with it for a while and then decided to file a claim. Ultimately, I wanted my story known.

The initial filing was simple enough, but writing the narrative about the abuse was not. At the time, my only scouting-related abuse memories involved my parents — even though I sensed more was buried underneath.

I spoke to several attorneys early on. Many referrals, many denials. I ended up navigating the process without legal counsel, which was frustrating at times and strangely empowering at others.

I knew nothing about bankruptcy proceedings or what the filing process entailed — which forms to complete, how to submit them, what the timeline looked like.

The BSA Settlement Trust, however, was extremely helpful. They responded promptly to every question. I was meticulous about following instructions and meeting deadlines.

So many people filed claims, and many didn't continue.

I know for me — during this process and even in therapy — when a horrific memory surfaces, the feeling is often, *"I've had enough. I can't do this anymore."* I've learned that in those moments, I need to step back, take a break, nurture myself, and decide later whether to continue.

And then the emotional cost began to surface.

Emotionally, the process has been both challenging and rewarding. The challenges came unexpectedly — more memories of specific scouting abuse incidents, each one taking an emotional toll. The reward came from freeing them from the abyss so they could finally heal.

Writing about the abuse in detail is reliving some of the most horrible chapters of my earliest existence. But I want to work through that part of my life and embrace a better one.

I have had intense fears of dying throughout this process. Those feelings are beyond uncomfortable.

Writing and talking about the very things that came with threats to my life is a big part of those fears. They don't disappear quickly. I have to work with them and reparent myself.

The fear remains until it finally releases. It's a slow process.

From the beginning, I shared with the Trust that I had been abused hundreds of times as a child. I certainly haven't had hundreds of specific memories — and as of writing this memoir, I estimate I've remembered between 50 and 75.

That isn't hundreds. The memories come when they come, go when they go, and integrate when they integrate. The healing work is draining.

I have had much support along the way.

A few weeks ago, I was meeting with my boss. During the meeting, I expressed my appreciation for my job and for how he manages and mentors. I thanked him for the flexibility and autonomy I've been given. As I was speaking, my eyes filled with tears and I started to cry. I said, "I wouldn't be able to do the work on myself these past few years without your support."

I have been blessed with amazing therapists. I've been with my current therapist for almost seven years. Years ago, I remember thinking that all the abuse I suffered as a child would be too much for him — or any therapist. I told him that.

He responded, "I'm not going anywhere."

I burst into tears.

These people are the angels in my life.

There was no one protecting me as a small boy in scouting while the abuse was happening. I was burdened with stuffing it all inside, never to be dealt with or shared.

This process has been painful but clarifying. A big lesson is that I am no longer the boy who had no protection. I am the adult who has support — and the ability — to heal.

The entire settlement process has become much more than a legal journey; it has become a catalyst for deep healing.

17

WHAT WAS I WANTING?

I have a very close friend I've checked in with throughout the last five years of the BSA settlement process. A few months ago, she asked me, "What are you wanting out of all of this?" I've thought about that question a lot as my case winds down and the process becomes less labor-intensive and less emotionally consuming.

What I was seeking has changed over the last five years. Initially, I wanted to tell my entire abuse story and have it heard without judgment. That was my first driving force.

I contacted several law firms early in the process. Many referrals, many denials. It was exhausting.

Eventually, I connected with a firm that wanted to hear my story before deciding whether to represent me.

One attorney was assigned to gather the facts. I was nervous talking to him. He was patient and respectful. The conversation took place over the phone.

He asked if I minded him taking notes. I told him, "Not at all, please do."

I began telling my sexual abuse story from beginning to end. I told him about the abuse by family members. I told him about the scouting incidents I had remembered up to that point. I became emotional several times.

At one point he said, "David, I am so sorry that all of that happened to you."

He listened to my entire story without judgment. He spent two hours on the phone with me.

When we wrapped up, I felt relieved and exhausted. I told him I had never shared my entire abuse story with anyone outside of therapy — only bits and pieces with a few very close friends.

I thanked him for listening.

I appreciated not hearing the comments I had heard from my immediate family in the past:

"Are you sure that happened?" "When are you going to be done with this?" "I just don't see how _______ could have done this."

Or the glazed-over look that said everything without saying anything.

Those responses frustrated me and brought up a lot of anger.

Therapy has taught me to be selective about who I share my story with. I've grown in that area.

Abusers — and those who protect them — often try to silence the ones who were abused.

The firm ultimately did not take my case, though they referred me to one or two others. I followed up, and no one took my case. Surprisingly, I was okay with that.

But the real test came later.

I had no intention of stopping the journey until I reached the lengthy questionnaire. I had to write extensively about every piece of the abuse involving scouting.

Once again, I made the decision to tell the whole story — to write about all of it. I wanted to provide context.

It took me months to finish the questionnaire. It was grueling because I began having additional memories — many memories. New memories of abuse by family members. More memories of abuse in scouting. One day I asked myself:

"Why am I continuing with this?"

I decided to continue because the truth — my truth — needs to be in the world.

I also had a small thought that maybe I would write about it someday. And as cliché or self-help-book-ish as it sounds, maybe the book could help someone know they are not alone.

I shared all of this in a letter to the Trust the day I submitted my questionnaire.

Today, when I think about my friend's question, my answer has expanded. I now ask myself:

"What do I want for myself?" "What do I want for other survivors?" "What do I want for society?"

For myself, I want to be at peace with my entire life and heal to the highest degree possible from what was done to me as a child. One thing I haven't mentioned is financial compensation. There could never be any amount of money that would undo or repair the physical, emotional, spiritual, and psychological wounds the abuse caused.

For other survivors, I want healing. I want them to have resources and access to the best trauma therapy possible. I want people to know they are not alone. I don't want anyone to go through what I endured — neither the abuse nor the reliving of it decades later. No child should ever experience this. And if they do, we must teach children that it is okay to talk to a trusted adult — and that we believe them, no matter what the abusers told them.

For society, I want this type of abuse to stop. I want statute-of-limitations laws to change in every state so survivors have a legal pathway to hold abusers accountable, even decades later.

Memories return in their own time. Abusers should not get away with the soul-murder of even one child.

As of the writing of this book, the Epstein situation continues to unfold with the release of more files — and it is horrific.

People need to take a hard look at what is being done to children — and how few perpetrators are ever held responsible. The injustice of impunity is staggering.

In my own life, not one person who sexually abused me as a child has ever admitted it or been held accountable. Some are still alive, living their lives without any legal consequences.

I wonder how many more children they may have abused over the decades.

Sharing my story — although challenging — is furthering my healing.

PART IV

REBUILDING

18

SEEKING HELP

I was twenty-six or twenty-seven years old, sitting in a twelve-step meeting for families of alcoholics.

My father was an alcoholic — a horrible person who abused me in many ways as a child. I had been attending Al-Anon meetings for years and found them helpful. I had walked to this particular meeting from my nearby apartment that night.

The meeting was in progress, people were sharing around the circle, and I was next. I began to speak — I don't remember the specifics — but I was sharing about some current life struggle.

Less than a minute into my sharing, a woman sitting directly across from me began to have a stroke. She vomited on herself and collapsed. I froze. Someone called 911 while others attended to her.

The woman sitting to my right said, "I hope it wasn't something you said." I know she meant it as a joke, but the comment freaked me out and unleashed a wave of fear and shame.

The ambulance arrived, and I left the meeting.

As I walked home in a deeply triggered and traumatized state, a chain of events began that catapulted me into a new world.

A series of snapshots and flashbacks appeared from my child-hood. One was a baby on a towel. It was me. Then came an overwhelming feeling of dread — and a realization I had never had before. In that moment, I knew I had been sexually abused as a child. It was intense as hell.

I was living with a woman at the time.

As soon as I got home, I opened the door and felt compelled to get into the shower. I needed to cleanse myself. I jumped in.

I felt horribly nauseous. I began to sob — deep, guttural sobs that went on and on. As I cried, clarity hit me even harder: it was my father. I will never forget that night.

I knew our household was dysfunctional growing up, but I would have sworn I had never been sexually abused.

After that night, I was driven to get help.

I knew of a support organization for women who had been sexually abused as children — I had even referred the woman I lived with to them months earlier. She had shared with me that she had been abused by her father.

I called the organization and learned they had recently started a men's group. It met once a week in Denver. I needed help to deal with this new, unmanageable truth.

Driving to the meeting for the first time, I became overwhelmingly nervous. I stopped at a convenience store, bought a few chocolate bars, and ate them on the way. I needed to numb myself. I parked outside of the meeting location. I waited. I couldn't go in. I drove around the block and then drove home.

For weeks, I thought about the meeting. Fear kept me from attending, but underneath the fear was a bubbling of deep emotional pain.

Eventually, I got up the nerve to drive there again. I parked, walked in, and attended my first meeting.

I felt at home in a way — every single man in the group had been sexually abused as a child, even the therapist.

The meeting was intense. They talked openly about the horrible things that had happened to them. I had never experienced anything like it.

I felt better for finally attending. After the meeting, I told one man it had taken me weeks to walk through the door. He said, "It took me months."

I was no longer alone. I continued with the group for quite some time. Being with this community of broken men was healing.

That was the beginning — but the road ahead was long.

I have seen many therapists and worked with many healing modalities: Cognitive Behavioral Therapy, Talk Therapy, Somatic Therapy, EMDR, Brainspotting, Couples Therapy, 12-Step groups, Internal Family Systems (IFS). The list is long — you name it, I tried it.

So much of the sexual abuse became lodged in my body.

I sought out complementary therapies as well: massage, acupuncture, Reiki, and others. Writing this list today feels overwhelming — I tried so many things hoping to be healed.

I remember one day visiting a somatic/talk therapist I had seen on and off. He was extremely talented, and I was experiencing enormous healing during that period.

One day, I was frustrated — angry that after all the years of work and all the modalities, I still wasn't "healed." I blurted out, "I want to find the book with the answer that will heal me."

I will never forget his response: "That book hasn't been written yet, David."

What works for one person may not work for another. What works for someone else may not work for me. Accepting that has been one of the most frustrating parts of recovering from childhood sexual abuse. There is no one-size-fits-all solution.

I have slowly learned to trust what I need in each moment. And honestly, sometimes I have no clue. It's an enormous challenge.

I previously mentioned some of the times and places where memories have surfaced. They also come at work, in churches, with friends, during naps, and when I'm home alone — everywhere. I can manage them better now, and that's growth.

For a long time, when memories surfaced, I would completely dissociate and my body would collapse. This happened in therapy several times. One day, as I began to dissociate, my therapist said, "David, look at me."

His voice anchored me. I looked at him — a safe, trusted adult — and immediately began to weep. I wasn't alone anymore. I was in the present, witnessing the memory rather than becoming that helpless boy again.

He said, "You don't have to do this alone, David."

The contrast between being isolated during the abuse and being supported in therapy has been profoundly healing.

I have seen many therapists and been in many groups. My healing has been slow, nonlinear, and dependent on safe, supportive environments.

When a memory hits me today, even when I'm alone, I am better able to comfort the small, wounded child inside who needs unconditional love and safety. I am rebuilding myself — with the help of others.

Rebuilding oneself is challenging when you are still trying to understand that you were once shattered.

19

UNTANGLING

My body went into freeze mode during the sexual abuse I endured as a child. I also dissociated, which took me out of feeling anything other than a huge void. The undoing, thawing, and healing have made reclaiming my life a long road back — and the work is ongoing.

I discovered *Waking the Tiger* by Peter Levine many years ago. It opened my mind to understanding trauma in a new way.

The book describes how animals sometimes freeze or "play dead" when a predator threatens them. When the threat is gone, the animal shakes — literally tremors — to release the trauma. That idea resonated deeply with me.

I started having involuntary body tremors shortly before discovering the book.

I wasn't sure what was happening. My body would shake or contort around my head and neck. I had been doing a lot of body work, and I was grateful for this unexpected unfolding — this strange, powerful healing gift.

I've experienced body tremors repeatedly over many years. They require a safe, relaxed setting, steady breathing, and sometimes coaching from a therapist.

My instinct is always to stop breathing — the same instinct I had during the abuse — so the gentle reminder to breathe is always welcome. It helps me surrender and let my body do what it needs to do.

This is extremely tough for a system that survived by freezing and dissociating.

When memories surface, they usually begin with discomfort or pain in a specific area of my body. Lately, it has been my upper body — neck, throat, back — which makes sense given the oral abuse memories I've been working through.

When the tremors come on, I often massage the back of my neck until I can surrender to them. Again, the breathing is everything. Breath is life.

Sometimes, while this is happening, I see or hear fragments of what happened during the original abuse. Sometimes I don't.

There are times I get stuck in my head, trying to figure out what is happening, what the memory is, what it means.

My therapist will gently remind me, "You don't have to figure it all out right now. Just let the body do what it wants to do. Breathe."

When I can surrender completely, the release passes more quickly. And always — keep breathing.

This is the opposite of what I did during the abuse: freezing, holding my breath, disappearing into dissociation. It is the slow unlearning of a survival stance.

Sometimes the memories come in waves. When that happens, it's tough, and I do my best to surrender to everything happening in my body.

After the tremoring — and sometimes during — the buried feelings come out: anger, rage, grief.

Mostly grief. And then I sob.

I've had tremors in one body area, in multiple areas, and full-body tremors. I'm exhausted afterward. But it is a gift to my body when I can do this work — and a gift to rest afterward. I believe this is the key to releasing trauma.

I've experienced the "felt sense" of body parts coming back to life after years of numbness.

I noticed it once with the bottoms of my feet. I was walking on floor tile and suddenly felt the texture and coolness beneath me. I hadn't realized how disconnected my feet were until I felt them again.

I still notice cool surfaces under my feet — even through shoes. I never felt life in my feet before.

I'm also recently able to sit still for longer periods and even sit cross-legged in a meditative position. Sitting still has been a lifelong challenge.

I had a recent revelation about how often my body's freeze response kicked in during the abuse. I was threatened repeatedly that I would be killed if I moved. The only survival choice was to freeze.

My brain learned that stillness equals danger — even death. So if I was always moving, always busy, I wouldn't die.

It isn't true, but it shows how childhood sexual abuse rewires a child's mind and creates lifelong consequences.

I am still learning that stillness does not equal death.

During massage and acupuncture sessions, a few trusted body workers have pointed out rope-like marks appearing around my arms or chest — marks that rise to the surface and then disappear.

One massage therapist once paused and asked, "David, were you tied up as a kid? Because there are rope marks appearing around your wrists."

I opened my eyes and looked. It was eerie — faint indentations circling both wrists. They disappeared shortly after the session. The memory was ready to rise and release.

Other body memories have surfaced too.

I've had sharp, debilitating pain in my anus throughout my life — body memories tied to the traumatic assault in New Mexico.

And after the coercive incident in Colorado, where the scout-master forced me into harming another scout, it became clear why any sexual activity involving penetration has felt dangerous to me — as if I'm hurting someone.

Healing from that will be lifelong. I am enraged by that trauma because it has had such lasting consequences. That single act happened over fifty years ago.

One of my biggest challenges is regaining sensation in my genitals. The entire area feels like a void. I've had erectile dysfunction for most of my adult life.

The emotional thawing is its own process. During the abuse, all my emotions froze. Many memories carry multiple emotions. Untangling them is overwhelming and exhausting — and necessary.

I've made enormous progress in feeling the once-frozen emotions. I've learned to grieve, to express anger safely, to experience joy more than ever before.

There are still struggles — especially with allowing good feelings to stay for more than a moment. I was frozen as a child, and I am thawing as an adult.

My body had been telling the story of my abusive childhood long before I ever could, and I've learned how my body wants to heal.

20

THE ME I WANT TO BE

"Who do I want to be now?"

It's interesting being older and asking myself this question. It's exciting, and it brings up a wide range of emotions.

The past is just that — the past. Although I've needed to revisit it to work through the trauma, I don't want to live there anymore. I don't want to forget it either, because it has shaped the person I am today.

There is grief and sadness for the young little David who didn't get to live and dream like many other children who had far less to endure. There will always be more to grieve. But I no longer need to let it consume me. That was an old default mode.

Often, it's one step forward and two steps back when memories arise. New memories push the pause button on living for a while. I need to accept those seeming setbacks while remembering that all the work now is moving me forward.

I am living more of the life I have always desired.

Time is a finite resource — forever valuable. It is important to no longer waste it. I need to choose to live fully each day.

Over the past few years, I've made a conscious effort to recognize

the type of energy people give off. I have far less tolerance for negativity and have eliminated some people from my life who are consistently negative and toxic.

Two such people are my mother and surviving brother. Their
denial, manipulation, negativity, and emotional abuse are things I no
longer choose to be around.

They are family — and they are very unhealthy people.

I deserved better as a child and had no choice then. Today, I am
an adult, and I *do* have a choice. Realizing this has been one of the
greatest gifts of healing.

It is a true blessing to choose the people I spend time with today.

I have strengthened my relationships with other family members
— the healthier ones, the ones who love and accept me unconditionally. The ones who talk about the difficult times and the wonderful
times. This has been a huge gift.

I have several very close friends, and I work to strengthen those
relationships. They inspire me in their own ways.

One friend I've known for many years lives in Las Vegas. I've
made a conscious effort to visit her at least once a year. We see shows,
eat at amazing restaurants, hang out, joke, laugh, bitch, moan, and
accept each other one hundred percent. We lovingly confront each
other. We have the most amazing time together. She is one of the
kindest humans I've ever met.

I want to be the kind of person my aunt and uncle modeled for
me as a kid. My uncle passed away a few years ago, and at his funeral
many people talked about how he always took them on drives.

He taught me how to drive, and we would talk during those
drives. He knew about my strained relationship with my mother.
Once, he pulled the car over and asked, "Dave, have you talked to
your mom?"

I said, "No."

He began, "You know, she's not—"

I interrupted him: "Gene, you don't know the whole story."

He paused and said, "You're right. I guess I should be talking to
your mother."

It was a beautiful moment — I set a boundary with a parental figure, and it was honored. That had never happened before in my life. It felt incredible. He never mentioned my mother again.

My uncle had a great sense of humor. We share that quality. He loved me unconditionally. My aunt loved me the same way. She volunteered at the church, helped neighbors, and is one of the kindest people in my life — and also very funny.

My aunt and uncle were married over sixty years before he died. I want to be more like them. Their example continues to guide me.

I want to embody, more deeply, the qualities my aunt, uncle, friends, coworkers, and mentors possess. I study these people.

I choose kindness today. I strive to be a better version of myself each day. I want to be a good friend.

At work, I want to be inspiring and a role model. I want to be a valuable addition to my community. I live in a great one — a place where people actually talk to each other.

I want to be respectful.

I want to experience more joy and laughter.

Recently, during a therapy session, things became very challenging. We took a short break, and something my therapist said struck me as funny. I started laughing — really laughing — and he joined in. It was beautiful and healing.

I want more humor in my life.

I love writing humor. I've participated in improvisation and acting for many years and love it, especially when comedy is involved. Incorporating more joy and humor is where I want my spirit to live.

I want to be the person who continues to go after my dreams and goals with confidence — not holding back.

I want to be the person whose life isn't defined by abuse, but the person remembered for living a kick-ass life with zero regrets.

After decades of surviving and healing, I'm finally living — and becoming the person I have always wanted to be.

I'm becoming my 2.0.

21

____

INTRODUCING COMPASSION

I was in my early forties and taking a medication I had been prescribed. I was having side effects and wanted to stop. I tried tapering off, but eventually decided to quit completely.

My digestive system reacted immediately.

It was very scary.

Eating became difficult. My skin turned ashen. I could take in very few liquids — mostly only water in the morning before attempting to eat anything. My body didn't want to take anything in.

I lived on peas and mashed potatoes.

This went on for about six months.

I lost about twenty pounds. Work became challenging. I was overly emotional and felt like I was dying. I could barely walk around the block in the morning without becoming exhausted — and this was shortly after waking up.

The tightness in my stomach was extreme. It felt like my entire digestive system was frozen.

I remember standing in the kitchen one morning, trying to drink a glass of water. The tightening got worse as I tried to swallow.

I became enraged.

I put the glass down. I made a fist with my left hand and started punching myself in the stomach.

I was angry, frustrated, and hating my stomach for betraying me.

I went to numerous doctors, and no one could figure out what was happening.

I truly thought I was dying.

The struggles continued, and I managed as best I could. One day, I had a rage attack. I went outside and tried to run down the street — and couldn't. My entire body was in a knot. My stomach completely frozen.

I screamed, "FUCK!"

It echoed down the street.

I walked home, went inside, collapsed onto the couch, and cried.

After I calmed down, a thought entered my mind:

"I wonder if what my body is doing has something to do with the sexual abuse that happened to me as a child?"

That moment cracked something open.

I had taken a break from therapy and support groups for a while, but after that rageful day, I decided to start attending another men's support group for survivors of childhood abuse.

I also returned to individual therapy.

All of this helped, but the process was slow. I could eat a little more — not much, but more. Liquids were still difficult.

Along that journey, I discovered Internal Family Systems (IFS), created by Richard Schwartz, PhD.

The way I understand IFS is that I have parts of myself inside stuck at different ages of development. During the sexual abuse, some of those younger parts froze. They shut down to survive.

Healing comes from working gently and compassionately with those wounded parts.

This resonated deeply. It was an aha moment.

I found an IFS therapist outside Boulder — a colleague of Richard Schwartz — and began to have results.

Through this work, I met buried parts of myself. I learned to give them voice. With guidance, I dialogued with younger versions of me — sometimes directly, sometimes through writing.

I've mentioned before that people I know who were sexually abused have all been affected differently.

For me, I've had to do an immense amount of work to get my nervous system back online. It gets triggered easily because I was so young when the abuse happened.

I began learning how to work with the most wounded younger parts — the Little Davids. I had names for them: Baby David, Age 5 David, Age 9 David, and so on.

They reminded me that the only thing they knew how to do during the abuse was run away and hide — meaning freeze and dissociate. They did this to stay alive.

Working with them taught me that I need to slow down, check in, and have compassion for those younger, wounded, frozen parts.

When I operate from curiosity and compassion — not fear or anger — I get results. My parts feel safe. My body thaws and relaxes.

I have to constantly remind myself that my body did what it needed to do to protect me from overwhelm and potential death.

About a year ago, I bought a small stuffed child online and named him Little David. He even has green eyes — like me.

Sometimes I sit him on a chair and talk to him. Then I switch chairs, put him on my lap, and respond internally as the younger part.

I've had memories surface during this work. I've had insights I couldn't have accessed any other way.

Deep feelings have surfaced too. During those times, I hold Little David and tell him what I wish I had heard as a child:

"You're safe." "I'm so sorry for what happened to you." "I will protect you." "You are brave."

This work is profound. I am learning to give the frozen young parts the love they never received.

I am giving them what they needed from a safe, loving adult.

I think back to the day in the kitchen when I was hitting my stomach — how I couldn't identify what was happening when my body shut down.

The only tools I had then were out-of-control emotions: anger, rage, frustration.

I didn't understand it was an inner call for help.

I have learned — and continue to learn — to have deep compassion and patience for the healing of these very young, frozen, but thawing parts of myself.

Those parts did what they had to do to survive the storm of sexual abuse.

I have had to learn that compassion and unconditional love become the bridge between the frozen younger parts and the healing adult I am becoming.

22

———————

FORGIVENESS

As a child raised in an abusive home and within the Catholic Church, I was taught to forgive. Reflecting back, I don't remember ever having the word specifically defined. I heard countless sermons urging parishioners to practice forgiveness, but never once did I hear a Forgiveness 101 talk.

I was an altar boy and attended many masses, yet I never heard anyone explain what forgiveness actually meant.

What sank into my youthful understanding was something I didn't believe in. I thought forgiveness meant forgetting — giving in to all the horrible things people do because "God forgives." You just go on as if nothing happened, even if what happened was morally wrong or illegal.

This created a deeply disempowering view of forgiveness.

Over the years I heard:

"You just need to forgive and get over it." "Let it go." "Holding onto resentment is like drinking poison and waiting for the other person to die." "Forgive and forget."

These phrases only caused deeper confusion, struggle, and frustration.

I developed a deep inner conflict between forgiving and feeling. I froze to survive the sexual abuse — in body and emotion. My emotions were denied, beaten down, and buried.

A big part of my healing has been learning to feel the frozen feelings when they resurface.

I once heard a phrase that resonated: *"You have to feel it to heal it."* I needed to feel what I never got to feel — anger, rage, grief — because not doing so would only cause further harm.

I need to allow those old, unexpressed emotions to come out, especially anger, rage, and deep grief.

I agree with the idea of "letting go," but I cannot let go of something I'm not aware of, something frozen, or something beaten into me. First, I need to be made aware. Next, I must feel it. Then process it. Then integrate it. Only then can I let it go.

And believe me — once that work is done, I *want* to let that shit go.

What I've discovered in recent years is that my first step in forgiveness is forgiving myself.

Especially during the challenging moments of my healing journey.

When questions arise like:

"Why is my body still frozen?" "Why am I not healing faster?" "Why did I forget the abuse?" "Why didn't I say no as a kid?" "Why does my throat constrict when I eat a banana?" "Why do I feel shame during sex?"

These are the moments when I need to slow down, listen without judgment, and comfort myself.

These are the youngest, most wounded inner voices — terrified and needing compassion. If I judge them or tell them to "get over it," I only cause further harm.

A big part of learning about trauma has been understanding that my body did what it needed to do to protect me and save my life. It was never my younger selves' fault.

And when anger and rage surface — even violent thoughts toward the abusers — I need to acknowledge those feelings and respond with understanding:

"I understand why you feel that way now, Young David. Thank you for feeling safe enough with me to share your rage."

Those moments are profoundly healing. This approach has helped me tremendously.

Forgiveness, to me, is not excusing sexual abuse. A big part of me feels that the sexual abuse of children is an unforgivable act — and I may never see it differently.

Forgiveness for me today begins with looking into every crevice of my early childhood and working with the most wounded parts of myself — the parts that believe they could have prevented the abuse.

I remind those parts that they were children. Sick adults were hurting them. There was no way they could have stopped it.

This is my ongoing forgiveness work.

I remind my younger selves that we cannot change what happened. What the adult part of me *can* do is heal, feel what arises, and respond to myself in new ways.

Self-forgiveness means:

Continuing my healing work. Setting strong boundaries with toxic people. Speaking the truth. Living an honest life. Being kind. Following my dreams. Inviting joy, happiness, and laughter into my life. Striving to be free of the past.

This is self-forgiveness in action.

And when I can practice this for myself, I can practice it with others.

Forgiveness has become less about the past and more about how I choose to live my life today.

23

SHIFTING

I was brainwashed by those in scouting who abused me. I was told, "You're a *faggoty* little Cub Scout." I was told, "I will kill you if you tell anyone." And after many of the sexual abuse incidents: "It didn't happen." "Nothing happened." And the worst, after I was forced to abuse my fellow scout and friend: "You are just like me now."

These messages sank in deeply while I was in a dissociated state. They destroyed my self-image, my confidence, and created internalized shame. I continue to work on shifting what was programmed into me decades ago.

The work I've done with healers, body workers, and therapists has invited a recent shift — first inside, then outwardly. I have thrived more in the last five years than at any other time in my life.

I pursued a long-held dream and earned a master's degree, graduating at the top of my class. I was the oldest cohort among my colleagues. I purchased my own home. I received a new job and have excelled in my work. I have a great job and an amazing boss. I am slowly returning to sports. I've had several plays published in the last two years. I have high-quality friends.

These are all examples of thriving — and I want to continue growing as a life thriver.

But thriving brings its own challenges.

It is difficult for me to allow myself to be present and feel good for an extended period. Often, when I feel joy, something inside says, "This will not last."

It's a direct hangover from the sexual abuse — because there was always a "next time."

Recently, during a group meditation, I heard something that helped me: "Be fearlessly present." I smiled when I heard it, and I smile now as I write this. A moment of joy.

When I look back on scouting and what my experience *should* have been, it should have been an environment of safety, curiosity, joy, and discovery. A place to bond with fellow scouts. A place where adult mentors modeled admirable qualities.

Instead, I was taught to mistrust myself and those supposed mentors. I was taught to protect pedophiles. I was taught to doubt the truth. I was taught that life is to be feared — in a setting that should have been joyful and inviting.

The core of what I was taught is shame.

Shame is the most horrible feeling I have ever experienced. It's like looking in the mirror and seeing yourself as a mistake — someone who doesn't belong on the planet, someone ugly to the core. Seeing yourself as a piece of shit.

I should have been encouraged to see myself as a beautiful creation. A gift to the world.

I work hard to shift my thinking and tell myself:

I am worthy. I deserve. I am beautiful. Life is good. I am grateful. I deserve joy. I belong.

This is easier said than done when you were programmed so young to hate yourself.

It takes work to untwist those feelings of despair while welcoming, appreciating, and staying in joy. Joy was paired with danger in scouting. It takes consistent practice to override that programming — and even after decades of therapy, it is slow progress.

Recently, I've noticed that the more I feel good, the more fear enters the picture.

Fear of living. Fear of dying. Fear of feeling good. Fear of getting ill. Fear. Fear. Fear.

It's as if my system believes positive feelings must be followed by negative consequences. It's frustrating.

I had a therapy session recently where things were going well — until fear showed up. I told my therapist, "I just want to make the fear smaller."

He responded, "What if you made yourself bigger?"

His comment struck me in an aha kind of way. I burst into laughter because it offered a complete 180-degree shift in thinking. It was brilliant — an invitation to expand my thinking, my programming, my life.

I cannot make fear go away. My therapist and I talk often about how fear can coexist with living bigger and having a good life.

Fear is not a bad thing — it can save my life. But I need to learn not to let fear *rule* my life. The type of fear I deal with is debilitating — the kind that keeps me from living.

One example: "Oh, I shouldn't visit my friend in California because the plane might crash." And then I make up a reason not to go.

Sexual abuse made me want to be small and unnoticed. My thinking was, "If I'm small enough, I won't be seen — and I won't be abused."

That thinking carried into many areas of my life and invited me to live small everywhere — even in the areas where I thrive. I am ready to say goodbye to that level of fear and work diligently to do so.

When I have long windows of growth and spend more time in the good, I am training myself to coexist with fear while living the life I want.

I am overcoming what abuse taught me — and that is healing.

Remembering my therapist's advice the day fear came to visit is a lesson I carry with me:

I slow down, breathe, and ask myself, "What if I made myself bigger?"

Shifting my thinking and actions is the work of reclaiming the parts of me that were shaped by fear.

24

WHY CONTINUE?

There are days when I wake up and my throat is tight, my neck hurts, my stomach is contracted, my chest is tight — and I know something is happening, though I'm not sure what. And all of this can happen after a decent night of sleep.

The day unfolds. I can be at work, at the gym, or at home, and suddenly I feel myself going away — dissociating. My stomach freezes, my chest tightens, and I'm back in a place I never asked to return to.

My body shuts down. I feel like I want to die. I can't think straight.

I'm having a memory.

It takes hours — sometimes days — to come back online.

These types of days suck.

During these despairing times, a question sometimes surfaces: **"Why did the sexual abuse happen to me?"**

This kind of setback used to swallow me whole. It was a loop with no exit. I could spend long periods spiraling in it, searching for the perfect philosophical or spiritual answer — "I am a better person because of the abuse."

And the wounded parts inside would respond, **"Fuck that shit!"**

I must meet myself where I am, with compassion on the rough days, and get curious by asking, **"What is it that I need right now?"**

The "Why me?" isn't wrong — it's human. And many times, I may never have the answer.

On another tough day, I remember being in my therapist's office, lying back on the couch. My body buzzing with nausea, thinking I might hurl at any moment, and having another horrible sexual abuse memory. I wanted to crawl out of my skin.

The memory came on full force and passed slowly. The session wound down and I felt like absolute shit.

I said to my therapist, "I don't know why I continue."

He turned it back to me, gently and curiously: **"Why do you continue, David?"**

A moment passed, and tears filled my eyes. I blurted out, **"I want a better life." "I continue because I want to heal."**

I left his office that day, and his question stayed with me.

Why do I continue?

I continue because I have a deep feeling that if I don't, the abusers win. And I will not let that happen.

It might seem like a strange reason, but it is a driver for me.

My thinking is: **"You fuckers may have thought you broke me. You didn't." "My spirit is strong, and my will to live — even during acts that could have killed me — is stronger than your cowardice." "That young boy at nine and ten was stronger than you abusive pieces of shit."**

I continue because I want and deserve a life that is mine. I continue because that wounded boy inside deserves someone to fight for his healing. I continue because stopping would mean letting the abuse define the rest of my life story.

My healing journey has had bumps in the road and moments when I wanted to stop.

But when I choose to continue, there are gifts.

On the other side of continuing, I experience deep self-discovery and growth. I have grown more during my decades of healing than I ever thought possible. I have discovered a new sense of curiosity about myself, others, and the world. I have discovered a deeper love and appreciation for myself and the people in my life. I have discovered my ongoing longing to grow, expand, and squeeze every ounce out of life.

Continuing the work is how I reclaim the life that was interrupted.

25

NURTURING LIFE MENTORS

Traveling through life believing I wouldn't live past the age of twenty-six created a mindset of not investing in people or deep, meaningful relationships. I never imagined a future beyond that young age.

I was filled with shame and didn't let myself be seen or known. I didn't understand this until decades into my healing, but those imprinted beliefs shaped everything — friendships, dating, and how I moved through the world.

My cousin Elise is one of my life mentors.

As kids, neither of us had the words to describe how we felt in the world, but we recognized something in each other — a knowing, a connection.

She was one of the first people who accepted me completely and made me feel seen without explanation.

We showed up for each other, both knowing our grandmother wasn't as fond of either of us as she was of the other grandkids. We laughed together. I used to put on magic shows for the family, and Elise would sell popcorn to our relatives.

Today, Elise is still a huge part of my life — the sister I never had.

We connected through pain, through feeling ostracized, through being made fun of as children. Today, we tell each other we love each other often. We laugh about the past. We cry together.

Elise is one of the most loving and caring people I know. She gives 1000% to her job and the meaningful work she does. She is a loving daughter, grandmother, friend, sister, and cousin.

She loves me to the core of my being and tells me so regularly. She has my back like few others. Thinking of her as I write this makes me smile. I admire so many of her human qualities.

My current boss is also a mentor. We share a similar work philosophy:

If a meeting isn't going to be productive, don't have it. If a task needs doing, do it now so it doesn't pile up later.

If I reach out to him, I rarely wait more than an hour for a reply. He appreciates my work and tells me so regularly. He connects me to others in the workplace.

He is a physician, highly specialized, and a mentor to residents. He encourages newer physicians to reach out to him for consults, even when he first meets them.

He supports my personal growth and commitment to it. He has a strong work-life balance. He gives me help when I ask for it. These seemingly simple things are big things in the workplace.

My current therapist is a role model.

He is a grand human being. His smile is genuine and infectious. He has passion for his work, and it fills the room.

There are days when I arrive feeling tender and wounded from the aftermath of the past, and he meets me with an unintrusive smile. It's grounding. It reminds me that joy is possible, even alongside the hard work.

The joyful and harmonious world he lives in attracts greater good into his life — a living example that the same is possible for me. He puts good into the world, and it comes back multiplied.

One of the greatest things about him is that he does his own work. He asks for feedback. He isn't married to his way being the only way. It is a partnership in healing.

He appreciates when I ask for help. I remember one session when gentle music was playing and I didn't like the song. I asked him to change it. He did. I didn't like the next one. He changed it again. And again. Until I liked the song.

I could have been shamed, ignored, or challenged — and I wasn't. I was accepted and supported.

I learned on a deep level that day that I could use my voice to ask for what I want — and receive it.

This is huge for a sexual abuse thriver.

One of the most challenging and rewarding parts of my healing has been getting to know myself more deeply.

I've also learned from people outside of therapy.

Several individuals I worked with retired this past year. What I honor about them is that they chose to pursue their passions, desires, wants, and needs later in life.

One newly retired friend said, "I want to travel with my husband more while we are both healthy." They truly love each other and have realized that work has its place, but it isn't the whole of life as we age.

Another retired friend is extremely creative — an actor, story-teller, mini-origami master, and ukulele player and teacher. I've had one lesson with him. His teaching style is inviting, supportive, and gentle — and he plays a kick-ass ukulele.

My other retired colleague is a person of color and a life mentor to many young people. He shares openly about his struggles and successes. He supports his mentees in pursuing their dreams.

He is one of the kindest souls I know — a joy to be around. He's the kind of person you can sit with in silence and feel better just being in his presence.

He is a master of saying no without apology — a great lesson in taking care of oneself without guilt or shame.

I have other friends and mentors. I learn from each of them how to manage and appreciate life. None of them fixed me. None of them rescued me. They model what is possible.

They show me how to live with integrity, kindness, boundaries, and joy. They help me grow into someone who can finally feel like he belongs.

All these mentors help me continue growing into the man I never believed I would live long enough to become.

PART V

WHAT NOW?

26

WHAT DOES HEALING LOOK LIKE?

I had zero awareness that I had been sexually abused — and then one day everything shifted, and that realization was anything but gentle.

I was walking along my life path, and then the ground caved in beneath me.

One day I thought I understood my past and my childhood, and the next day everything I believed about myself, my family, and my history was rearranged.

Overwhelm swept over me like a storm. I didn't know where to turn. I didn't know who I was anymore. I felt like shit.

My mind ricocheted from one thought to another. The chatter was too much to handle. Massive confusion. The feelings clumped together when they surfaced, and if one feeling outlasted the others, it was fear.

I doubted the possibility that life would ever be anything but a struggle.

I needed help in any and every form available.

A big part of my healing has been exploring different modalities. Every new modality felt like a lifetime. I'd walk into acupuncture or somatic therapy thinking, *"Maybe this is the one that will finally heal me.*" I'd make a little progress, and then the fantasy of a single cure dissolved.

What remained was the truth: **healing is a mosaic, not an instant miracle.**

I made significant progress in safe groups facilitated by talented therapists. Hearing another person's story — especially when it echoed mine — let me know I wasn't alone. Even those with different narratives but similar emotional aftermath helped me. The groups taught me how to build safe community.

Body work helped at times, and at other times it didn't. When I was in memory hell, I didn't want anyone touching me — it was too triggering.

Writing, creativity, and art helped in a deeply subconscious way — an indirect path inward and an outlet.

Physical exercise helped immensely: walking, running, hiking, swimming, biking, lifting weights.

And individual therapy with a highly experienced trauma therapist has been essential. Finding that kind of therapist takes work and research.

I've ultimately learned that I need to trust my gut about what to do — and what not to do — as I continue to heal. My gut choices are becoming stronger and more accurate now.

The abuse taught me to doubt my gut. Healing is teaching me the opposite.

Through all of this, I've often imagined what true, comprehensive support could look like.

I've dreamed of a multidisciplinary childhood trauma treatment center for adults — a place where a highly skilled team designs an individualized healing menu for each person.

One person's healing menu might include individual therapy, an improvisation class, and swimming for a few months. The next month they might add weekly body work, an art class, and maybe the vacation of their dreams.

The plan would be monitored and adjusted over time, allowing each person the opportunity for deep healing.

My healing journey has been one I never could have imagined. I never knew healing would take so long. I've had to make peace with the fact that I will never be fully "healed."

But I've experienced deep degrees of healing in many areas of my life, and for that I am grateful.

I think of something I heard in a healing group many years ago:

"First it gets better, then it gets worse, then it gets real, then it gets different, and then it gets really different."

I am living in "really different" today.

Currently, I work with a therapist, follow an exercise program, explore breathwork, get acupuncture, write creatively, spend time with friends and in solitude, practice gratitude, and try to eat well and get restful sleep.

Sleep has always been a challenge, and in the last year I've made a conscious effort to improve it. It comes back to trusting the part of me that feels self-directed.

I'm not saying this is *the* healing program — guaranteed to heal anyone from childhood sexual abuse. It's simply my current focus and, it may shift. It's a tough journey, especially when new memories surface.

I've had many scouting abuse memories in the last few years, and they make healing tough — but the tough times are temporary. I know that now.

Healing, for me, is no longer a destination. It's building a new relationship — with my body, my memories, my younger selves, and the life I'm building today.

Some days it's challenging. Some days it's absolutely amazing. Every day, I am becoming more of the me I was created to be.

Healing is less about fixing the past and more about living fully in the present.

27

———

SHARING MY STORY

I have written portions of my sexual abuse story over the decades, and I always stopped. It was too much — too much reliving. I put it away, hoping the horror of my childhood would disappear.

It never did.

Revisiting the truth brought up too much unhealed shame, too thick to face. Fear surfaced and became overwhelming.

But healing changes the way I see myself today. And hiding my story isn't protecting me anymore — it's hiding the truth and protecting the people who hurt me.

I have done more healing work, and I continue to work. I have done extensive work on self-acceptance. I know today that I am perfect alongside my human imperfections. I accept all my healing, even when there are setbacks.

I remind myself — and the younger, still-healing parts of me — that those who abused me in and outside of scouting were sick, twisted, unsafe people. They were manipulative, coercive individuals in positions of power who used their status to harm a child.

I see this type of abuse today as one of the most cowardly acts anyone could commit. It is always a no-win situation for the small child.

I wrote a play entitled *Brother by Brother*, which was recently published. It is a fiction piece inspired by true events and addresses childhood sexual abuse. I wrote the play to bring truth to light — to show the devastation caused in families when the truth stays in the darkness.

There is a scene in the play where one brother paints a truthful picture of a specific sexual abuse memory to the other sibling. I've had many readings of the play by theater professionals and community members.

One professional told me the climactic scene was "too graphic" and should be removed. I said, "No," and kept it in.

I thought about his comment many times. What he was really saying was that the play was "too real."

The truth is sometimes graphic. Sexual abuse is graphic. Sanitizing it only protects the abusers.

Sharing the truth through art has been very healing.

I have shared my lived sexual abuse story with the wrong people from time to time. It has been trial and error. People often do not want to hear what happened. They respond with:

"No!" "That didn't happen." "People aren't that evil."

Hearing others deny my truth can be retraumatizing.

I have a few close friends I do share my story with, and I've learned to take responsibility by checking in before I share. Early in my healing, I wanted to tell everyone. I've learned discernment.

And then there are moments when sharing my story opens doors instead of closing them.

I had coffee with a friend today and told him about this memoir and the scouting sexual abuse. He shared with me an abuse incident he knew of within an organization he was involved in. The board wanted to avoid addressing it, afraid that exposing it would bring negative attention locally and nationally.

My friend took a stand against the board members. He called

them out for protecting someone's immoral behavior. Because of his willingness to speak out, the individual was terminated.

I appreciated his advocacy — his willingness to address what no one wants to address.

People need to stop protecting abusers and start holding them accountable. The climate around this type of thinking must change. Inaction turns seemingly innocent bystanders into accomplices to horrible crimes.

Several of the sexual abusers who perpetrated me are still alive. One lives in Colorado. Neither, to my knowledge, has ever been held accountable. I wonder how many children they abused after me.

Most of the family members who sexually abused me are dead. They took the secret with them to the grave — trying to sweep it under the rug even in death.

I share my story because silence is how sexual abuse continues. Speaking and sharing the truth is how it stops.

Sharing my story is an enormous part of reclaiming the life that was taken from me.

28

A PROMISE: A LETTER
TO MY CUB SCOUT SELF

I have always wanted to be a parent. I am coming to the stark realization that this will most likely never happen, and it saddens me.

I was talking to my therapist one day and mentioned this, and then suddenly stopped myself and said, "Wait a minute. I *am* a parent — to myself."

After that realization, I thought: why not write a letter to my younger self...

Dear David,

I'm writing to you because you carried far too much alone as a child and young scout, and you deserve to hear from me — your older self, an adult who finally sees you clearly.

I want to make you a promise, well, several of them — promises that should have been made to you long ago.

First, I want you to know how incredibly brave you are.

Over several years, you've trusted me with memories that were too big, too frightening, and too painful for you to hold. You let me see what happened to you in scouting, and I am deeply touched by your trust. What you shared was real. It did happen. And none of it — not one single second — was ever your fault.

Those men were adults who abused their power. They were manipulative, coercive, and deeply sick. You were a child. A good child. A creative, funny, sensitive, bright child who deserved protection and nurturing, not harm.

What they did was cowardly, and the shame belongs to them — not to you.

I want to help you reclaim the parts of your life that froze during those years. I want to explore your dreams with you — the ones you tucked away when surviving became more important than imagining and creating.

I remember how much you loved to swim; how free you felt in the water. I remember your silly stories, your wild imagination, your humor that could light up a room. Remember how your aunt used to laugh with us when we were being silly? She still does.

We're writing again now — together. Stories, plays, and movie scripts. I promise you we'll keep creating. You were always a storyteller. I'm just helping you find your voice again.

I know how much you love animals; how gentle you are with them. They see your goodness. They always have. We'll keep making space for that part of you — the part that feels safe with soft fur, warm eyes, and unconditional love.

I know how the abuse made you shut down — how it taught you to be afraid of people, of joy, of being seen, of experiencing every ounce of your body.

I'm here now to help you rediscover wonder. To help you play again. To help you be goofy and free. We're doing improv, we're doing theater — things that let you move and laugh and breathe. And we'll do more, so much more...

Here is my promise to you:

I will be your safe adult. I will listen to you. I will believe you. I will protect you. I will tell you the truth. I will never ask you to take care of me — that was never your job. I will let you grow at your own pace. I will give you space when you need it and closeness when you want it. I will honor your "no" every single time. I will remind you, again and again, that you matter. You belong. You are loved. You are no one's object. You are no one's secret. You are no one's shame.

You are a boy who deserved safety, joy, and protection — and you have those things now.

I'm here. I'm not going anywhere.

We get to build the rest of this life together, and I promise you it can be filled with laughter, creativity, connection, and dreams that finally get to grow.

Thank you for trusting me. Thank you for surviving. Thank you for letting me love you.

With all my heart,

David — Your Adult Self

29

SERVICE

Sexual abuse taught me many things, and one of the biggest was to stay small — everywhere.

As healing continues, I keep exploring how I can live larger and be of service in my daily life. Participating in life this way helps me expand and reclaim space in the world.

I am of service in my work life, and I often think about what it means to extend that into my community and in the world.

I work with healthcare learners and professionals — medical students, nursing students, interns, physician assistants, doctors, surgeons, and others. I help them take stock of their professionalism and communication with patients, colleagues, and coworkers. I often say, "How can you help someone if you can't speak to them in a caring and compassionate manner?"

I've been contemplating writing a book about the methods, techniques, and tools I use with the people I coach — a way to give my work a wider reach.

Years ago, I trained a physician to become a communication coach for medical students. One day he said, "David, you should write down what you teach and put it in a book." He planted the seed.

I've dabbled. I've talked about it with colleagues. And still — no book.

A few years ago, a colleague said, "Either you write the book or it dies with you." That hit me hard — in a good way.

I've made progress in the last two years, but something still blocks me from finishing it. I wonder if this is another place where I'm still staying small – another echo of the abuse.

It's time to burst out of that bubble. To do it despite the fear. Writing that book would be an act of service — and an act of self-liberation.

Before I was aware of much of the scouting abuse, I served as the chair of a nonprofit that provided services for adults who had been sexually abused as children. I shared my story and talked about the healing I had done up to that point. I had practice telling my story during retreats and workshops.

The first time I told my story in public, my voice constricted and shook — and I kept telling it anyway. I was sharing the secret. The feeling eventually passed. I was not alone. I was in a supportive space.

I did this several times and was eventually invited to tell my story — along with other survivors — to a group of United States military service members by their general.

Service doesn't always look big. Sometimes it's quiet, simple, and close to home.

I've discovered recently that I experience extreme joy in being of service in small ways.

I live in a community with amazing neighbors. When I moved in, I was proactive in meeting all of them — something I had never done before.

Four of us share a cement back porch area where leaves collect near our back doors. The leaves build up, and honestly, it drives me nuts because I track them inside.

One day I was sweeping up the leaves and decided to just keep going. I swept around my door, then my next-door neighbor's, then the others, even the far neighbor's door.

I felt a quiet joy – being of service in a simple way. I didn't need to point it out to anyone. It was just nice to see everything clean.

For so long, my energy went into surviving. The secret of the abuse was an enormous energy drain. Sweeping those leaves was a contrast — a sign that I now have more energy for others after clearing out life's secrets.

My service to others has expanded, and I find joy in being in that space.

There are other small ways I am of service to people and organizations, and I prefer to keep those private. I do them for no outward gain or recognition.

It all feeds my soul and makes my heart smile.

Being sexually abused taught me a twisted set of rules and survival strategies. It planted in my developing brain a distorted way of seeing people. It made me distrust and avoid others instead of embracing them and being of service.

In scouting, I thought I would be taught how to be a good person — how to help others. Instead, those leaders taught me the opposite: how to hurt, use, and take from others. I wanted no part of it, even though I didn't understand why at the time.

And healing work continues to shift how I serve others.

I have competed in and organized sporting events in the past. There was a running race about a year ago and the marathon portion of the race passed my home out to the turnaround point and then came back past my place a few miles from the finish line.

I decided to run the 5K that day, which I did. I thought afterwards I would make my way home and cheer on the marathoners. I got home and rehydrated. I went outside and cheered on the marathoners for about an hour.

I went back inside, rested for a bit and then came back outside and cheered on another wave of runners. There were thousands of runners. I took another break, went inside and then came back out again.

I was tired, the sun was getting warmer, and I was ready to go back inside and relax for the rest of the day. It was right at that moment that one of the race course marshals' came by and said, "There's seven more runners." I decided to stay outside and cheer every single one of them on.

As the very last runner approached, I clapped and cheered him on, "Way to go." "You're almost there." He looked exhausted and with much effort squeezed out, "I don't know why I signed up for this shit." I smiled and replied, "Well, you have much less of a distance to go compared to when you started." He smiled back and said, "That's true, thanks." I watched as he continued on after our brief human to human interaction.

I was glad I decided to wait for him.

As I crossed the street toward my home, I began to wonder why this person had decided to run a marathon. Was he challenging himself for one reason or another? Was he wanting to be in better health? Was he running in someone's honor? Was he possibly an abuse survivor?" Tears filled my eyes as I thought about my own healing journey. I thought about how having a single abuse memory — and surviving the reliving of it — is a marathon within itself.

I thought about how I was of service to that man and other runners during the marathon that day and in doing so how I had been given a gift. The gift of seeing how far I have come in my own healing.

Being of service is how I continue to heal forward. It's one of the ways I reclaim my life — and what was taken from me.

30

BEING VS. DOING

Doing has kept me alive — at least that's what I used to think.

I was a heavy doer for most of my earlier life. Doing. Doing. Doing. Doing many things. Many things at once. The busier, the better.

What I have learned — and continue to relearn — is that the more I stay busy, the less time I have to look at myself.

Slowing down, in my mind, was equated with death.

Because underneath all the busyness and doing was something horrible I didn't want to see, even though I wasn't sure exactly what it was at the time.

A little over twenty years ago, I became very ill. I went from being a competitive runner to losing twenty pounds in a very short period. I could barely eat. I thought I was going to die.

I was forced into *being*.

One of the hardest things for me to do in my life is to be okay being myself.

I was told who I was by the abusers and brainwashed along the way. I identified with being a piece of shit — with whatever they told me I was. If I wasn't what they told me, I was nobody. And when the "you" is beaten and threatened out of you, anything is better than nothing.

The truth is, I didn't want to be any of what I was told — but I was too weak to be something different.

Being forced to abuse my neighborhood friend and fellow scout as a boy did an excruciating amount of damage. It destroyed any chance of finding myself during those years. It damaged my psyche.

The final words the scoutmaster said to me after the forced trauma — *"You are just like me now"* — created a core shame identity that I was as horrible as the person forcing me to hurt someone else.

From that day forward, I believed I was evil, horrible, sick. I had done the unthinkable, the unspeakable. And it was so bad that I blanked it out for over fifty years.

But the internalized shame stayed and unknowingly drove my life.

Stillness, no doubt, would bring it all up again.

So I got busy. Really busy. I worked and worked.

Becoming ill — losing all that weight, having my body shut down — forced me to confront the demons hiding deep inside. The ones programmed into me. The ones running my inner sense of being. The ones hiding the shame.

I was forced to slow down, rest, and work extensively on healing.

Where does one start to remove internal shame and brainwashing from decades ago?

I tried affirmations. They didn't work. Saying "I am worthy" was no match for the "You're a piece of shit" voice embedded in my core.

I tried to meditate. I couldn't cross my legs. My hips were too tight. Sitting in a chair made it worse. My mind spun with horrible thoughts.

I tried yoga and had some success — but I framed it as exercise and competed with myself, burying my thoughts in doing instead of being.

Mild running and swimming helped because I didn't have to sit still — but they were still forms of staying busy.

Journaling helped. Individual therapy helped. Slowly, I was inching toward being.

The hardest part was trying to change something programmed so deeply inside me when I didn't even know where it was born. What happened to make such an awful internal feeling appear? What happened to me to make me this way?

When I had the forced perpetration memory and worked — and worked — and worked at being present with the feelings, the anger, the rage, the grief, I noticed a shift. It is overwhelming to feel emotions buried so deeply.

The implicit damage became explicit — and then I could finally process portions of it.

I am still working on that specific memory and it will take much more therapy to fully process it.

I've noticed lately that I can sit and meditate in a cross-legged position longer than ever before. I can be at home alone with myself and not have to get up every two or three minutes because I literally cannot sit with myself.

This huge gift is the result of committing to the hard work — trusting the healing journey. Trusting that not knowing is part of the journey. Showing up anyway and doing my best to be present.

Lately, when practicing this level of mindful presence, fear steps in — overwhelming fear. The fear that I will die. It tends to be relentless until it isn't.

Recently, during therapy, I had a revelation and blurted out, **"Stillness does not equal death."**

My therapist responded, "Yes!"

You see, I was told by my scoutmaster that if I ever told anyone about the abuse, he would kill me. As a child, I couldn't sit with that thought, so I tucked it away. But it stayed underneath the surface, ruling my life.

It finally came out in a way I could connect the dots — because I am finally in a place where I can deal with the depth of the fear.

I work at being mindful.

About ten years ago, I was on a retreat with men who had been sexually abused, and we did a mindful eating exercise — being completely present with each bite. It was an amazing experience.

The more present I was, the less I wanted to eat. I had stuffed my feelings with food and candy as a kid.

I spend time hiking and running in Boulder. I love looking at the Flatiron Mountains — majestic and grounding. I notice them differently now. I feel my feet hitting the pavement. I look at the grass and trees as I pass them. Nature and its beauty steady me.

And this is all on a good day.

I try to bring myself to the now and experience the present moment. Some days it is easier than others. My being practice is ongoing.

I am learning to be with myself more each day — and being is no longer the enemy to be feared.

Being is how I continue to reclaim the life that doing was protecting me from.

31

LIVING

Two friends have a young boy, now approaching age three, and a few years ago the wife said to me, "I'm not trying to push my son on you, David, but I think you need to spend some time together. You two have similar energy."

Her insight made me smile. I felt honored — and I took her up on the offer.

I've had many opportunities to spend time with my friends and their son. It is a complete joy to watch him play. I notice how free he is when he runs around — a direct contrast to how my body felt as a child: rigid, guarded, burdened.

Watching him reminds me that my body *can* relax, that freedom is possible.

I watch him laugh, cry, pout, and express anger — all within minutes. This is what I love about young children. They move through emotions with ease, and it inspires me. It's like the universe is showing me what is possible, even now, at an older age.

When we live freely in our bodies, there is a flow — the ability to feel the full span of emotions and move from one to another in their own time. I see that as living in the arena of emotional flow, and I desire that life today.

My childhood was shaped by survival mode. Shutting down, freezing, awkwardness — that was my normal. As I continue to heal and free up frozen memories, the backlog of tangled emotions surfaces.

I am freer today to feel an array of emotions. And when I relax, I can dabble in that emotionally flowing arena. It is an amazing place to be.

I am not like my friends' young son — but I am getting better every day, and I'm grateful for his mentorship.

As I write this, I'm smiling because *this* is living. It's also a reminder that I am more in my body today than at any other time in my life. I never experienced the freedom to emote as a child.

Exploring what I missed as a child is one way I live more and there are others.

I love to travel, and I do so on occasion. I enjoy trips with friends and trips by myself. I love visiting places I've never been. Traveling alone teaches me how to enjoy my own company — how to deepen my friendship with myself.

My favorite music is country music. A few years ago, I treated myself to a trip to Nashville. I had never been, and it was the perfect destination.

I was working on a writing project at the time. I'd get up early and write, then work out in the hotel gym, then go explore — museums, landmarks, music halls, restaurants, gift shops. In the afternoon, I'd write again. At night, I'd treat myself to live music.

I met and connected with many strangers. I remember sitting next to a woman at The Grand Ole Opry. We struck up a conversation, and I learned she was from another country — her first time in North America, her first time in Nashville. Two strangers, side by side, having separate and shared new experiences.

It was a magnificent trip. I enjoyed every minute. It was truly a living experience.

I learned that I could trust myself in a new place — and have a lot of fun.

I took another trip and volunteered at a retreat center in Hawaii. I camped in a tent for an entire month. It took four or five days to adjust, and by the end, I didn't want to leave.

I met people from all over the world. Working in the kitchen, greeting and serving food to guests and volunteers, I got to know many people. I remember sitting at a table chatting with a visiting couple for hours. When we finished, they thanked me for connecting with them.

I swam in the ocean, talked to locals, took day trips, had the best locally made ice cream, went to my first ecstatic dance, toured the island.

It was one of the best experiences of my life.

I learned that exploring the world can be an amazing adventure. I learned that there are fascinating people on the planet. I learned that not everyone is out to hurt me. I learned that like attracts like — good attracts good when I am present to my life.

I learned that I am a kind and likable person — nothing like what my abusers told me. This is healing.

These experiences taught me what living actually feels like.

Living today means:

- Embracing new experiences
- Speaking more freely and openly with others
- Giving without expectation
- Choosing to be a good person
- Telling the truth
- Caring for myself
- Treating myself with gentleness
- Appreciating who I am
- Releasing what no longer serves me
- Staying committed to growth
- Making space for play
- Laughing often
- Being with people I love — and telling them
- Following my passions and lifelong dreams, knowing it is never too late

I will continue to expand and add to this list every day.

I also know I have setbacks — the one-step-forward, two-steps-back days. These usually come when I'm working through tough sexual abuse memories or other life challenges.

Someone once said to me, "I used to have bad years. Now I have bad days." I never forgot that. It's true for me.

The gift of healing is being able to live — and knowing that challenges do not have to become a lifetime.

Healing hasn't made my life perfect. It has made life *possible*.

Living is the part of life I never believed I'd reach — and I am doing that very thing.

32

PLAY AND LAUGHTER

I spent another evening with my two friends and their young son. They had just bought a new swing set and set it up in the backyard. We were all outside together.

Their child was running around the swing set, laughing hysterically. We joined in — running, being silly, laughing with him. His laughter kept building and building, becoming more infectious by the second. I felt lighter in my body as I ran around the swing set, soaking in the joy with him and my friends.

It was the ultimate sense of freedom.

As a child, the most consistent play I remember was when I stayed with my aunt, uncle, and cousins in Kansas. I felt that same sense of lightness, freedom, and spontaneity in my friends' backyard with their son.

When I think about my home growing up, the only specific memories of feeling free while playing or laughing were alone with my dog. I'm sure it happened in other ways, but nothing stands out. I was too busy being on guard to survive.

Scouting was the same — an environment full of dissociation. I didn't know play as a child. It wasn't safe.

Having suffered childhood sexual abuse creates a challenge in this arena later in life. The aftermath plays out until we feel safe enough, healed enough, and make the bold decision that it's time to do things differently.

Abuse teaches unhealthy limits, confinement, and protection — the opposite of play.

During the COVID shutdown, I facilitated an online Improvisational Comedy class for healthcare professionals. We met once a week to play and laugh together. The need came from the isolation everyone was feeling. Our gatherings provided community and connection — something we were all longing for.

We met for well over a year, playing a multitude of improvisational games. The safety and trust we built allowed us to cut loose and find relief from isolation through shared silliness.

Eventually, the fear of looking foolish evaporated. The play dissolved the physical isolation. We reached a point where we shared one collective group mind of silliness. It was community at its best.

Play shows up in many forms in my life today.

I have a friend I hang out with on occasion, and we are complete goofs together — joking, inviting each other into spontaneous silliness. We make up bizarre characters on the spot, creating little vignettes that almost always lead to guttural laughter. Our humor complements each other.

My friend told me recently, "I don't laugh this much with anyone." It felt good to hear — and I agreed.

I believe in the healing power of laughter. There is nothing better than an extended belly laugh. I need to remind myself to seek out more outlets for play and laughter.

A few years ago, during a wave of sexual abuse memories, I prescribed myself some art therapy. I decided to write a play — a silly, stupid comedy just for me. I didn't care if anything happened with it. My only goal was to make myself laugh while working on it.

I wrote a stage play about the theater. It was set in a fictitious mountain town where there had never been a murder — until suddenly there were many, and no one could solve them. The story centered around quirky townspeople.

A cardinal rule in playwriting is, "Never write a play about the theater if you want it to go anywhere." I didn't care. Who said that anyway? I trusted my gut and wrote the play I wanted to write.

Working on it was an absolute joy. I wanted to create the most stupid, silly play ever written about the theater. Knowing it would go nowhere freed me completely. I laughed out loud many times while creating it.

The process reminded me that joy and laughter were still inside me, waiting. It was one of the best writing experiences of my life.

I never thought anything would happen with it. And then, a few years later, a play publisher contacted me and offered to publish it. It was published in March 2025 with a very long title: **Never in a Small Town: The Wheeler Community Theatre Murders.**

Joy is an inside job. When I can feel it internally, I can express it outwardly. This is healing on a grand scale.

Abuse is often about isolation, and being alone can be triggering. Learning to enjoy my own company in solitude is beautiful.

I don't remember ever laughing alone in my room as a kid. I was isolating to survive.

As I get older, I know that lightness, joy, and laughter are more valuable than ever.

I recently started facilitating improvisation again with a few healthcare colleagues, and it is a joy to gather, play, and laugh with them.

I used to go to the animal shelter regularly and play with the animals. I haven't done that in a while — and I need to do things like this more often.

Participating in any type of play with safe people — where we don't have to edit ourselves — is an invitation to free and heal our souls. I've never believed play is frivolous. It is freedom.

33

REFLECTIONS ON THE
BSA SETTLEMENT

The BSA settlement process became a mirror, showing me who I have become. I never expected to learn so much about myself.

Learning to trust myself more deeply has been a lifelong journey.

Being taken advantage of as a child by many adults implanted mistrust not only in others, but in myself. After being abused by the scoutmaster, I was continuously told:

"It didn't happen." "Nothing happened." "I will kill you if you ever tell anyone."

These comments invite extreme self-doubt. They wire a child's brain to never trust himself. They distort and twist the truth.

I have committed to living a truthful life.

I remember hearing years ago, "When you tell the truth, you never have to remember anything." Although I couldn't speak the truth as a kid, I developed a sixth sense that saved my life then — and has served me ever since.

I have a deep sense of knowing when something is off, whether in myself or another person. As I've healed, I've learned to trust that sense more.

I was referred to a physical therapist by a renowned healthcare provider who understood the aftereffects of childhood trauma. The physical therapist worked with individuals who had suffered complex trauma. I was lucky to work with him for nearly a year.

At first, I didn't understand his methods. The first visit, he didn't touch me. The second visit, he didn't touch me either. I was bothered — I wanted the magical body maneuver that would heal me.

At the end of the second visit, he typed something into the electronic record and said, "There is what I type in here, and then there is what we talk about." I picked up on the politics of healthcare and insurance. I thought maybe he was a kind of shaman. I decided to come back.

Before the third visit, I resolved that if there wasn't hands-on work, I wouldn't return.

During that visit, he had me get on the massage table and close my eyes. He began walking around the room, and as he did, I felt something in my left lower abdomen — my epicenter of abuse — tracking him like a laser beam.

It was incredible. Whatever it was inside my body, it was following his every movement. Every single movement.

When the session ended, I told him, "My body is tracking you." He responded, "I know. I'm teaching your body to trust me."

It was profound. He told me this was essential if he was ever going to help me.

As the visits progressed, there was hands-on work. My body learned to trust him. I learned how to tell a body worker what felt good, what was too much, what was working, what wasn't. It taught me that my instincts weren't paranoia — they were wisdom.

Since that day, I have learned more deeply to trust myself, and that same trust in my instincts guided me through the settlement process.

I worked through the BSA settlement process without an attorney.

Part of the process included writing an extensive narrative about the scouting sexual abuse. It was extremely important to paint the entire picture of my childhood abuse inside and outside of scouting — to provide a frame of reference for the extent of the trauma.

I trusted myself that this was the correct approach, even though the settlement focused only on abuse that happened in scouting.

I shared that there were hundreds of abuse incidents throughout my childhood, and that once I start working on the abuse, more memories surface. I also shared that during my nearly two years as a scout, there was a huge gap of unaccounted time — a signal that more abuse likely happened.

I continued to update the Trust every time new memories surfaced. And it happened more than once.

Writing the narrative — and additional ones — was like walking back into the fire, a fire I knew would grow — but I did it on my terms. That was empowering and healing.

I included a letter stating that I welcomed a deposition or anything else they needed. I had nothing to hide anymore.

Several months later, an interview under oath was requested. I had been hiding secrets for so long that I welcomed the interview.

I was nervous when the day arrived, but I knew I was strong. All I had to do was tell the truth.

The interview began. I took an oath. Soon after, I became extremely emotional. I was talking about things that happened decades ago, and waves of grief came and went.

The interviewer asked several times, "Mr. Jensen, would you like to take a break?" I didn't. I wanted my truth out there.

I answered all questions honestly. Many answers were, "I do not know," or "I do not remember."

My scouting sexual abuse story didn't flow easily from beginning to end. I dissociated many times during the actual abuse. There were things I couldn't remember.

But I remembered the two abusers' names when the memories surfaced, and I shared them. I shared the threatening comments. Those details were coded in my mind.

Having never had a voice — literally or figuratively — is something I've worked hard to overcome. Being orally raped repeatedly and brainwashed shut down my voice completely.

The interviewer was respectful and professional. I was proud of myself when it was over. Speaking the truth out loud felt like reclaiming something that had been stolen from me.

I know today to trust sexual abuse memories more than ever.

I learned during the process that I didn't need an attorney. I became my own advocate — a stronger, healthier adult. When I felt unsure or overwhelmed, I took a break and returned when I was ready.

As the process progressed, I trusted myself more and more.

I learned how strong that small boy was to survive so much abuse. I learned that my spirit is extremely resilient.

I learned that I'm a pretty cool adult.

The settlement process didn't just ask me to remember. It asked me to trust myself — and I did.

It also became another step in reclaiming the voice that had been silenced decades ago.

34

THRIVING

I have never been a fan of labels. "Victim" and "Survivor" are not who I am. Those words feel disempowering to me today. I have fought hard and long during my recovery to move past those identifiers.

The last thing I want my legacy to be is: "David survived horrible sexual abuse as a child." Or, "He was a sexual abuse victim and part of the BSA Settlement."

That is not the legacy I want to leave.

My word of choice is **thrive.**

Thriving is the action I now take to honor the abused child who could never imagine such a life. My goal for the rest of my life is to thrive — to make up for all the lost years.

It is a battle when I get sucked back into surviving and victimhood. It usually happens when memories surface. The feeling of wanting to die is always challenging, but it has happened enough now that I can usually recognize it as memory time. Never fun, always work — but today I can be more present with the message.

It is a call for help from a young and deeply wounded part of me.

I had a huge breakthrough in therapy three or four years ago during a memory. It began with body tremors, then specific details surfaced, then dissociation. This is usually where the depths of wanting to die show up — a horrible feeling that feels like it will never end.

But it does end. And it did that day.

On the other side of the memory, I blurted out, **"I want to live."**

My therapist time-stamped the shift with me. It was monumental — a moment that changed the trajectory of my life.

Since that day, I've tried to nurture that voice and honor it by taking more steps toward thriving.

What does thriving mean to me?

Thriving means waking up after a restful sleep and greeting the mystery of each day with curiosity. Preparing myself for an amazing day filled with enriching experiences.

I take more time in the morning now. I drink three glasses of warm water — the first with lime or lemon. I greet my animals, feed them, brush them. I enjoy a morning writing session. I savor a cup of tea or coffee. Then I usually head to the gym. After that, another writing session focused on a current project. Then I dive into the workday — emails, administrative tasks, training preparation.

I love one-on-one time with select friends — coffee or lunch, deeper conversations, real connection. I appreciate the surroundings of where I live. I'm blessed to live in a community where neighbors talk to each other. I take time to greet them — and their pets.

Animals are one of the biggest blessings in my life. Their unconditional love is healing. I welcome any arena where I can experience more unconditional love.

I cherish pursuing my lifelong dreams in acting, playwriting, and improvisation. I push myself to grow in those worlds. I continue to write stupid, mindless comedies because they make me laugh out loud. The stupider, the better.

During graduate school, I spent time analyzing stage plays that translated well to film. I try to create those types of works now. One dream I've had for years is to create one big hit for the stage that translates well to the screen. I've made more space in my life for that possibility.

It's no longer about fame or fortune. If it happens, it happens. If it doesn't, I'm okay with that. Life on life's terms.

Earlier in my life, I wanted to be a millionaire by my twenties. Today, I want to be comfortable. A car that runs well. A comfortable place to live. Enough money to not worry — but no need to hoard millions while others struggle.

Managing my finances responsibly and having extra funds at the end of each month is how I thrive. Barely scraping by mirrors the programming that kept me small.

I enjoy helping people who are struggling — food, a nurturing gift — without enabling. I strive to be fully human and a good person. I want to add to life and leave the world better. I want to be known as someone who spoke truth, even when it was hard to hear.

I'm not a big meditator in the traditional sense. It used to be impossible for me to sit still. I'm getting better. I often have deep insights while running.

I'm not religious — religion was used against me as a child. But I consider myself spiritual. I believe I am part of something good, something larger than myself, something that has my best interest at heart. I live knowing this today.

I love spending time with safe, unconditionally loving family members — and that circle is larger than ever.

There are more ways I will continue to explore and discover how to thrive, and I embrace all of them.

I am living more of the life I fought for — a life I continue to build every day, a life I intend to live fully.

Thriving is the life I never believed I could have — and one I choose more each and every day.

35

SOLITUDE AND COMMUNITY

Being in community was dangerous for me as a kid, even though I longed for it.

I was hurt in a church community as a child during scouting. I was sexually abused in the basement of the church where our troop gathered. My abuse happened while events were happening upstairs — while other adults and scouts were present.

This fact is baffling.

When abuse happens inside a community, it doesn't just break trust — it breaks belonging.

The aftermath of that abuse has made me wary when exploring and engaging in community.

Spiritual communities and churches are extremely triggering for me. After my divorce, I found a non-denominational church where I felt comfortable and attended for several years. It was healing for a time.

One night, while taking a class at the church, I had a sexual abuse memory. I felt myself dissociate. A fog overtook my mind. I felt nauseous. It was frightening to suddenly feel unsafe in a place where I had felt so safe.

Looking back, it makes sense — our scout meetings were in a

church, often at night. Here I was in a safe church one minute, and the next, a memory arose.

It freaked me out, and I quit attending. Although I've been back, I no longer attend regularly.

This type of aftermath saddens and angers me.

The safest communities for me today are my work colleagues, close friends, the theater community, the gym and fitness community, and the comedy community.

I want to expand my involvement into other safe communities and actively look for new ones.

I'm currently looking for a volunteer opportunity with an organization that aligns with my core values.

I used to have a strong yoga practice and connected deeply with the people and instructors. The studio closed during COVID, and I'm committed to finding a new yoga community.

There was a meditation community I enjoyed years ago, and I recently reengaged with that group. Twenty years later, it's still led by the same individual. I've attended for the past month and even cried during my first return. This group meets in a church — and so far, so good.

I'm also interested in finding a men's drumming community. I was introduced to drumming during a healing retreat once, and it was powerful.

I'm drawn to communities that focus on living, growing, and appreciating life — without feeling like a cult.

I never knew how much damage is done when someone is sexually abused *inside* a community — especially one that should have provided support and safety.

Scouting was supposed to be about connection. Instead, it taught me that connection means danger.

Many communities invite vulnerability, and I need to feel completely safe when that is the case. The cost of community betrayal has led to hypervigilance. I need to be patient with myself.

Community should be about safety, support, and belonging — an invitation to be with others at one's own level of comfort.

After my first oral abuse memory with the scoutmaster downstairs, I remember sitting upstairs at the table with the rest of the scouts. That feeling of total fear, isolation, and aloneness while sitting in community scarred me for life.

I work hard to comfort the young boy inside who had such a life-altering experience.

Being seen in life is important. Feeling like my life contributes to the pack in a healthy way is essential to growth. All of that was disrupted during the repeated sexual abuse.

Being seen is essential — without judgment, coercion, or threats.

Solitude and community may seem like they don't play together, but I believe they do.

Healing has shown me that I don't have to choose one or the other.

I was isolated by the abusers. I was abused, brainwashed, and taught to hate myself. I followed that by isolating to hide the shame and avoid being seen — hoping it would keep me safe from being abused again.

My healing and forward focus are about learning to accept and love myself more deeply.

One of the biggest things I'm learning is how to appreciate my own company. And appreciating my own company requires solitude.

Solitude — not isolation. They are two very different experiences.

In solitude, I get to nurture and know myself on a deeper level. It is a place where I can restore and expand while supporting myself.

In solitude today, I reparent and rebuild myself. When I can do that, I am more authentic when I bring myself to community.

This inner work makes community safer.

After my divorce, I had a rough time being alone. I became so busy that I hid out in various communities. It was what I needed at the time. I was hurting too much to be alone. The aloneness would have triggered more sexual abuse memories and the abandonment I suffered as a child.

Today, I am becoming increasingly comfortable with myself — and I enjoy it.

This is a huge gift and deeply healing. I see now how much of it is an inside-out job.

When I accept and love myself — all of myself — I feel safer, stronger, and more me when I participate in community.

Healing is teaching me that solitude and community are not opposites — they are partners.

In solitude, I learn who I am. In community, I get to share what I've discovered.

36

APPRECIATING LIFE

Sexual abuse created lifelong wounds and impacted me in countless ways. But on my never-ending healing journey, a new clarity has been emerging — a clarity about appreciating life.

In 2019, I was working through deep abuse memories with a new therapist. I was also rehearsing a play with some of my favorite actors and a director I cherish. Being in a moving, beautiful play at that time helped ground me. It reminded me that I could still do something I loved with safe people.

One day during rehearsal, my phone rang. A friend told me that my best friend was in the hospital and likely going to die soon. Shock — like a ton of bricks to the face. What was I supposed to do in that tender moment?

I told him I'd get to the hospital as soon as I could. I informed the director and cast, and they supported me in whatever I chose. I stayed a little longer, then left for the hospital.

I drove nervously, grounding myself with deep breaths. I also felt blessed that I could go see him.

When I arrived, the friend who had called me greeted me outside the hospital room and updated me. We went in together and were met by my friend's mother and sister.

His sister said, "David is here."

My friend wasn't speaking; his eyes were closed. He raised one eyebrow and nodded slightly.

He knew I was there.

I stayed by his bedside for several hours. I didn't know whether to leave or stay. I had never been in this situation before. We talked, shared stories, and I decided to leave — but for some reason, I didn't. Something told me to stay.

I agreed to bring his sister coffee the next morning. Still, I didn't leave. We kept sharing stories.

I told them about a trip my friend and I had taken to Spain years earlier — how the Spanish I learned in school didn't work so well there.

Suddenly, something shifted in the room. We all stood up and gathered around him. We held hands.

Within less than a minute, my friend passed peacefully away.

It was beautifully horrific.

I had never been with someone I loved so deeply at the moment they died. It was calm. It was simple. And he was gone.

We all cried.

I was honored to speak at his funeral. I talked about friendship and broke down many times, then regained my composure and continued.

We had swum together as teammates for years. We traveled the world. We swam in four Olympic pools. We camped, biked, challenged each other, laughed together, loved each other — unconditionally.

He had a gentle soul. He taught me that you don't need to chase big things in life — you just need to be a good human.

His death was devastating. After he died, I questioned life and how unfair it can be. Why the fuck do younger people have to die before they should? Fuck cancer.

All these thoughts swirled inside me then — and still do. He was one of the kindest humans I've ever known.

His death reminded me about life — about living fully.

A short time before he passed, we had gone camping. After setting up our tents, something amazing happened: A deer walked right into our camp, between our tents. We froze. The deer came closer — within three feet.

Three gentle souls, sharing silence. It was profound.

I think about that day often. I appreciate every second I spent with him.

His death pushed me toward something I had always wanted to do: pursue further studies. I applied to graduate school and was accepted at the perfect program for me. I dedicated my studies to his memory.

My final project was a screenplay about two best friends — one dies, and leaves the other with an assignment: **Go after every dream we shared as kids.** Live. Do the things you're afraid to do. Get on with it. **Live the fuck out of your life.**

I graduated at the top of my class.

My life journey now is about appreciating life in whatever form it arrives.

I appreciate my life more every day and know how fragile it is — as is every life on the planet. On a good day, I can keep this in mind and treat others with kindness and respect.

None of us know when our last day will be. It scares me to write that. It scares the shit out of me.

But today, I am alive.

A little over a year ago in therapy, I had a revelation. I used to say, "I have to do this work." One day I said it aloud, and my therapist smiled — maybe even raised an eyebrow.

I paused, then said, "I *get* to do this work."

That was a big shift. I don't have to do anything I don't want to as an adult. I am in charge of my life today.

I am grateful to work on myself — to become a better human. I continue to open in body, mind, and spirit. I heal more deeply when I do the work.

My friend's death taught me how fragile life is. Healing is teaching me how precious living truly is.

His death broke my heart — and it also opened it to living and appreciating life.

37

ONGOING COMPASSION

One of the most challenging parts of my journey — and the most rewarding — has been developing deeper, ongoing compassion for myself. As I've worked intentionally, compassion flows more freely now, though being consistent with it is still a practice. I'm learning to notice when I need more of this gift.

When I look back at my younger years, my ability to show compassion was very limited.

I showed compassion to my pets. I worried about my dog being outside in the winter. I remember asking one day if he could sleep inside and being surprised when the answer was yes.

My compassion for my dog was authentic.

But I had no real compassion for myself. And when it came to others, compassion was forced — if it existed at all.

I wasn't having compassion modeled for me by the adults most present in my life.

The more I learn about early childhood sexual trauma and how it affects the body, mind, and spirit, the more clearly I see why compassion is essential to pass on to children.

I offer it today by comforting my younger wounded parts, reparenting, expressing my needs, being honest with others, embracing failures as lessons, letting go of self-judgment, trusting my feelings, accepting imperfections, validating memories, and setting strong boundaries with toxic people and environments.

I want to touch on a few of these areas.

Healing has created a shift. Big shifts come when I become more aware of what was done to me as a child, feel it, and then let it go. It is a slow process.

When I work through a memory, there is often a void — a space where I get to choose what to put back in its place.

One void I've worked hard to overcome centers around expressing my needs.

Recently, during body work, I asked the practitioner to support my neck more — and then asked if they could move it slowly side to side. I trusted myself. I asked for what I needed.

This was huge because it involved my body — and a part of my body that is overly sensitive due to the sexual abuse that happened there as a child. Afterward, the therapist thanked me for asking for what I wanted.

It was empowering and deeply healing. This seemingly small victory was huge.

In the past, I had no clue who I was or what I needed, especially regarding my own body. My body as a child was forced and manipulated to meet the sick needs of adults who were supposed to protect me and teach me about agency and autonomy.

The biggest and most frustrating challenge revolves around sexuality. I have so much old wounding and shame around sex. A big part of me still thinks anything sexual is bad or dangerous.

I'm still working to identify my sexual needs, wants, and desires. I need to be patient here — and have compassion for the youngest, most wounded parts of myself.

Another place compassion shows up is in reparenting.

I am constantly learning and practicing reparenting. A clue that an old wound is present is when I feel extremely overwhelmed. It's usually a signal that a younger part is triggered and full of fear — a part that wants to run the show.

During overwhelm, I need to put the brakes on, slow down, and check in. It's hard work because there is usually a whirlwind of emotions and thoughts all tangled together. Deep breaths help.

Once I slow down, I can check in with my younger self — through journaling or dialoguing — and things begin to untwist. It's usually a part of me that was terrorized and wants to be heard and comforted.

Sometimes I visualize holding the small boy I once was — the boy who had no one to go to during or after the abuse. Being able to do this often brings immediate comfort. Other times, it doesn't.

During overwhelming moments, I need to exercise even more compassion — and sometimes take a hard stop. If I can't calm the frightened parts, I take a nap. The overwhelm becomes too much.

Reparenting the younger Me's is some of the hardest work I've ever done. When I can deeply connect with and comfort those old wounds, the results compound on all the previous healing.

The reward is deeper healing and integration.

Another area I continue to work on is reframing failure.

As a child, I never wanted to spend time honing my talents — and that carried into adulthood. My wounded inner dialogue used to say:

"What's the use?" "I'm not going to be around that long anyway."

Those comments come from a brutalized place.

Today, I'm learning — and relearning — that permanence takes time. Dreams, goals, recovery, healing, relationships — they all take time.

And there is still time.

I am alive today and worth the investment.

I recently heard a cliché line in a cheesy movie: **"If you don't believe in yourself, no one will."** It landed deeply for the first time.

As a small boy, I had magical thinking — that if I were perfect enough, I wouldn't have been abused. Not true. I had no chance. The abusers were giants, and I was set up to fail every time.

As an adult, I invite looking silly and imperfect. I am not perfect. No one is.

This is newer thinking after internalizing a twisted perfectionism as a child.

I offer myself compassion when a young part gets triggered while pursuing new dreams — especially old frozen dreams. If I feel the need to be perfect right away, that's an old wound.

Success lives inside failure. We get better slowly, over time.

I'm developing deeper compassion and acceptance for myself during abuse memories that involve emotional overload. So many emotions wrapped up together — frozen as one.

The survivor part of me always wants to figure out *why* so much is coming up at once.

My therapist reminds me: **"Just be present."**

Present with what's happening in my body. Let that pass. Then be present with the emotion that follows.

I don't need to get in my head and figure out the why.

He always says, "We can worry about all of that later."

The more present I am with a body memory or feeling, the more quickly it passes. I've been able to do more of this lately — a huge breakthrough. It's healing. It takes patience and compassion.

Boundary-setting around toxic people and environments is one of the biggest ways I show myself compassion.

Today, I avoid these situations because they no longer feel comforting. I use the word comforting because as a kid, abuse was familiar — I made it the comfortable.

Now, when something feels off or toxic, I back away. The pull into the vortex is gone.

That is healing in action.

This is one of the greatest ways I show compassion to myself.

Ongoing Compassion — for myself and others — is one of the biggest gifts I've received by committing to healing the wounds of the past.

PART VI

LEGACY

38

LOVE

Love is one of the most powerful forces on the planet, and I've spent much of my life trying to understand what love truly is.

So much of my healing has been unlearning the distorted versions of love I was taught in childhood.

During my early life, "love" came with conditions, confusion, and harm. I was sexually abused and then told I was loved or praised as a "good cub scout." Those contradictions twisted the meaning of the word in my developing mind.

As I look forward and think about the legacy I want to leave, I also look back at the places where I first felt the kind of love I now believe in — unconditional love.

I think of the pets I had as a child, especially my dog running up to me, tail wagging, offering comfort without asking anything in return.

I think of my aunt and uncle, who accepted me, protected me, fed me, held me, played with me, taught me to drive, and gave me a safe place to sleep. Uninterrupted sleep. To this day, when I visit their home in Kansas, I sleep better. Those were the moments that showed me what love could be.

I think of teachers who encouraged me, challenged me, and saw potential in me. I wonder how many of them sensed I needed extra love beneath my frozen exterior.

I think of my swim coach, who provided a safe haven and pushed me to grow.

These were people who modeled real love, even when I didn't fully understand it.

I have learned much about love on my healing journey.

A big part of love is treating it as a verb. Love is something we *do*. When our actions align with our words, love becomes authentic.

When it comes to interactions with other humans, unconditional love is beautiful when it's present. It's loving without conditions, judgment, or expectations. Doing something kind for someone without wanting to be found out — and smiling inside because the act has no strings attached.

Unconditional love connects us as humans.

I believe love has the power to heal.

Replacing internal shame and self-hate with unconditional love heals my wounded soul and the brokenness of the past.

Love is sacred — and it is our birthright.

As I learn more about unconditional love and self-compassion, I see how they complement each other. Two superpowers working together.

A therapist once gave me a self-love assignment during a difficult time. She told me to place one hand over my heart so I could feel my heartbeat, and the other over my diaphragm to belly breathe. "Close your eyes," she said, "and feel your heart beating and your breath moving."

I tried it that night.

I settled in and followed her instructions. After a short time, I began thinking about the miracle of a heartbeat — how it is life. Then I focused on my breath, slow and steady.

I began to cry. Then sob.

Feeling my heartbeat and breath together, I had a thought: **"I'm a miracle."**

It was beautiful. That simple exercise was an invitation to love myself unconditionally and more deeply. It was profound. It opened a door.

I began contemplating other ways to love myself.

I show myself love in my body when I eat when I'm hungry, when I eat slowly and mindfully so I don't stuff my feelings. I show myself love when I rest when I'm tired. I show it when I exercise to strengthen my body.

I show myself love at work by not overworking, setting boundaries, taking breaks, saying no, and appreciating my contributions.

Having grown up with an unconditional-love deficit, I need to remember to fill my tank first. I cannot save any other car on the road if my own tank is empty.

I have the capacity today to appreciate and love others because I've spent the time filling my own tank. This has been a big shift — and it feels good.

I show others love by complimenting them, being present, helping, offering a hug while respecting boundaries, listening without giving advice, accepting people as they are, and not expecting them to change.

I show love to strangers by smiling, holding a door, giving anonymously, and other small acts.

As I continue to heal the wounded parts inside, I practice telling my younger self:

"You don't have to earn the right to exist." "You matter simply because you are here." "You are perfect just as you are." "I believe the horrible things you tell me happened to you, and I am here to listen, to hold you, and to reparent you at your pace." "I am not going anywhere."

Along with these messages, I want to expand my self-love practice — yoga, creative endeavors, adventurous vacations, joining additional safe communities, cooking healthy meals, reading inspiring books, spending more time with cherished friends, and dreaming bigger.

I am learning that the power of love is endless.

39

DREAMS

I want my legacy to be one where I went after — and achieved — many of my lifelong dreams.

When I think back to childhood, I remember sitting in my aunt and uncle's living room, watching a movie on cable television. The movie was *Liar's Moon* with Matt Dillon and Cindy Fisher. I watched it over and over that summer. It resonated with me in a way I couldn't explain and in ways I could now. Something inside me lit up as I watched the actors and the story unfold.

That experience time-stamped a dream: I wanted to use my creativity to tell stories.

I didn't know how, but I felt it in my body — I wanted to create narratives that mattered.

Recently, a friend asked me over coffee what a dream of mine would be today. I told him I've always wanted to have one big hit in my lifetime, however it shows up. Ideally something I've written.

There is huge value in storytelling. Stories teach, touch, explore, invite change, and move people.

I've written in many forms — screenplays, stage plays, short stories, and now a memoir.

I'm most moved when someone shares their life and I connect

with those who have been in the depths of despair and overcome obstacles.

I've attempted to write my sexual abuse story many times and always stopped. It became too overwhelming.

Writing this memoir has surprised me. Not once have I felt overwhelmed enough to stop. It's a lot to write about, but I've taken it step by step.

I share some of my childhood abuse in this book, but not all of it — and that has helped. I narrowed the focus: before scouting, during scouting, and after. What my life is today. What I envision for the future.

I've enjoyed reflecting on my healing journey and remembering key moments. There have been breakthroughs and pivotal shifts, and I look forward to many more.

It brings me joy to put energy into rewriting my life story — today, tomorrow, and for the future. Rewriting means consciously focusing on the newer me while integrating the benefits of healing.

I doubt I will ever be 100% healed from the damage done to me as an innocent kid. But I no longer need to let the abuse define my entire life.

The new story I choose to live is about dreaming big dreams and being more present each day. I can do this because I've cleared out large amounts of hidden trauma, secrets, and pain.

I am no longer consumed by the abuse I didn't even know happened. I feel freer — and grateful.

And the more I heal, the more space I have to dream.

I've achieved many lifelong dreams in the last five years.

I've explored getting to know myself on a core level, and I want to do more of that — discovering what I like, dislike, my strengths, weaknesses, passions.

I currently own my fourth guitar and have never learned to play. I'm not sure why I keep acquiring the same instrument without moving forward. It's time to enroll in lessons and learn to play the dang thing.

I still struggle with claiming a consistent spiritual practice and continue to dabble. I continue working toward the level of fitness I had before a wave of sexual abuse body memories hit. I've made great progress this past year.

I have community, and I want to participate in more safe communities that align with my values.

I would love an unconditionally loving and supportive relationship unlike anything I've experienced — and I'm okay if I don't have that. I love myself more than ever today.

My new story is about attracting what works for my life and dreams — and moving away from what doesn't.

My new life is also about accepting and letting go of certain dreams.

I always wanted children. I had foster children for about six months years ago. I would still love to have my own, and I've accepted that it may not happen.

When all is said and done, I want to have lived a life with no regrets — one I am proud of.

I am proud that my life story has been about speaking truth and standing tall in that truth regarding the sexual abuse I suffered at the hands of a scout volunteer, a scoutmaster, and members of my immediate family.

I have silenced the room with my truth over the years. My truth-telling honors the younger parts of me who never had a voice.

I will no longer be part of the secret.

One last dream of mine is to touch people's lives in a way that they are better off having known me — even if I never know it.

Many people along my path have enriched me in countless ways. Several of them appear in this book. These individuals are the angels who saved me and shaped the man I am today.

A dream I had as a child was to know that I mattered.

I know today that my life matters. It mattered before the abuse, during the abuse, and after. Every life matters.

40

HOPE

Hope is the topic I want to end this book with. During the most difficult times of life, hope can feel impossible.

During the horrific sexual abuse I endured as a child, my default was to go away — to dissociate. There was the before, the after, and the black hole of terror in between.

I remember what was said to me before, and I remember what was said afterward — the threats, the shame, the command to keep the secret.

But the act itself was a void.

I want to talk about the void, that black hole of terror, because something important happened in there.

Yes, my body shut down — and something else was happening too.

I have struggled my entire life with accepting the idea of a loving God, or even the existence of God in any form. I put spirituality in that same bucket for a very long time.

For years I could not accept that any God could let a child be sexually abused. If God is all-powerful and everywhere, why the fuck didn't he, she, or it intervene?

Why?

Years ago, after the Twin Towers collapsed in New York City, I was at the gym. I walked into the locker room and saw the news on. A reporter was interviewing the late Reverend Jesse Jackson and asked:

"Why did God allow this tragedy to happen to all those innocent people? Why didn't God intervene?"

I stopped and listened.

Reverend Jackson said, "I don't know... What I do know is we see God in people and how they are responding to others in New York City."

I began to cry.

In that instant, a new seed was planted.

Standing there in the locker room, I began to reshape my thinking about who or what God is, what God isn't, and what I do believe.

I thought, "Maybe all the people helping each other — first responders, neighbors, doctors, citizens — maybe that is God in action."

My next thought: "Maybe I've expected too much from a God."

As a child, I didn't have a framework for a God who doesn't intervene but still holds us somehow.

In Chapter 18, I shared my first abuse memory and what happened that night I attended the Al-Anon meeting after the woman had a stroke. I walked home, jumped into the shower, crying and nauseous.

What I didn't mention is that something else happened before the memory passed.

I heard something.

I don't know from whom or from where.

A calm, soothing, loving voice.

As I stood in that tiny shower, broken and sobbing, I heard:

"Everything will be okay."

I've thought about the strangeness of what I heard that night for many years. I didn't understand until recently.

"Everything will be okay."

A little over a year ago, during therapy, another scouting abuse memory surfaced. Never pleasant. Afterward, I was talking with my therapist and a new revelation came to me. I said:

"During all the abuse, although I didn't believe it at the time, I wasn't alone. Something was there, protecting me from dying. If there wasn't, I would have surely died."

"Something was there."

My therapist smiled.

That day was another monumental shift.

Recently, I had the same insight again — deeper this time. A reminder.

Something was happening in that black hole of terror while I was being horribly abused.

I was being protected.

The wisdom of my body shut down parts of me in order to save my life. The memory got filed away until I was able to deal with it. All of that was operating together.

It was something larger than me.

"Everything will be okay."

It was a feeling. It was comforting. And, it was confusing.

Call it what you will.

Where am I today with the big life questions...

What or who is God? I have no clue.

But when I think about the void — the black hole of terror, the dissociation, what was happening in there — I now believe some greater wisdom in the universe allowed me to disappear so I could survive to be here today.

It happened every time the sexual abuse happened. During the scouting abuse. During the family abuse.

Every time. Every single time.

And afterward...

I lived my life. I functioned as best I could for many years.

Looking back now:

I have traveled. I have met people. I have worked a multitude of jobs. I have made mistakes. I have found therapy. I have kept going.

Sometimes I took long breaks before I could go near the black hole of terror again.

I have learned so much about myself — what happened, how my body protected me then, and how it protects me now.

I have learned that deeper healing is possible.

Complete healing? I don't know.

But I love and accept myself today more than ever. I accept my life today. I have great people in my life. I have achieved lifelong dreams. I have overcome many challenges. And I have more I want to do.

I have more healing work to do. More dreams to fulfill. More desires to explore.

And I have hope.

All of what I listed above — all of it together — is part of something much bigger than me.

And I am part of it.

And that's pretty damn cool.

I hope that every person who has ever been sexually abused finds healing. My wish for every reader of this book is that you find something that feeds your passion and go after it.

Be kind. Love yourself. Love others. Show your love with actions. Find your safe community. Know that life is precious.

I wish all of this for every soul.

Healing is challenging and rewarding. *I get to work on myself today.* I'm worth it.

I wish you many blessings on your life journey.

And when times are tough — No matter what you think. No matter what you feel. You are not alone.

Hope is not the end of my story, but another beginning.

David Jensen

EPILOGUE

As I reach the end of this book, I find myself thinking less about what happened to me and more about the unseen threads that carried me through it. There were moments in my life when I felt completely alone, moments when the world went dark and silent, and yet — something kept me here. Something kept me breathing. Something kept me moving forward even when I didn't know why.

I don't pretend to understand what that something is. I don't need to.

What I know now is that there is a presence — a wisdom, a current, a quiet force, a spark — that has been with me in ways I couldn't recognize until much later. It was there in the black hole of terror. It was there in the dissociation that protected me. It was there in the people who showed up at exactly the right time. It was there in the voice that whispered, *Everything will be okay.*

Maybe that presence is God. Maybe it's the universe. The stars. Mountains. Oceans. Maybe it's the human spirit refusing to give up. Maybe it's all these things woven together.

What matters to me today is that I am part of something larger than the pain I lived through. Larger than the secrets I carried. Larger than the story I once believed about myself. I am connected — to myself, to people, to love, to healing, to possibility, to the quiet mystery that holds all of us.

Writing this memoir has been a way of honoring the boy I was, the man I became, and the soul I am still discovering. A way of saying: *I am here. I survived. I am still becoming.*

If you are reading this and carrying your own wounds, I want you to know that whatever you call the force that kept you alive — strength, spirit, intuition, grace, luck, God, or something unnamed — it is real. It is yours. It has never left you.

You are held in ways you may not yet understand. You are guided in ways you may not always see. You are part of something bigger than your pain, bigger than your past, bigger than the story you were given.

As for me, I will keep listening for that quiet voice. I will keep following the pull toward healing, toward love, toward the life that feels true. I will keep trusting that the same presence that carried me through the darkest moments of childhood will continue to walk with me into whatever comes next.

— David Jensen

ACKNOWLEDGMENTS

To everyone who offered me an ear, a hand, a breath, a moment of stillness — thank you. Healing is not something I did alone, and it is ongoing. It happens during therapy and in the quiet spaces between conversations, in solitude, in the warmth of friendship, in the gentle presence of people, and in community with those who love me unconditionally. To the teachers, coaches, mentors, and colleagues who encouraged my voice and trusted my truth: your belief helped me step into the light. To the survivors whose stories brushed against mine, whose courage echoed in my own healing — I honor you. We are connected in ways words can barely hold. To the friends who brought laughter back into my life, who reminded me that joy is not a luxury but a birthright — you helped me remember who I am. And to the child I once was: you carried the weight of silence for far too long. This book is the sound of that silence breaking.

RESOURCES

If anything in this book stirred memories, questions, or emotions that feel heavy to carry alone, I hope you'll reach toward the kind of support that feels right for your life. Healing can take many forms—through trusted people, skilled professionals, community, or practices that help you feel grounded and seen. You deserve care that meets you gently, wherever you are on your own path.

ABOUT THE AUTHOR

David Jensen is a writer and healthcare communication specialist whose work centers on relationship-building, curiosity, narrative, self-reflection, compassion, and clarity. He holds an MFA in Screen-writing and Playwriting and has spent decades helping clinicians, educators, and learners communicate with greater ease, empathy, and skill.

A lifelong storyteller, David brings honesty, truth-telling, and emotional insight to his creative work. He lives in Colorado, where he continues to write, teach, and build community rooted in healing, creativity, and hope.

Thank you for reading this story and staying with me through the parts that were hard to write and, I imagine, sometimes hard to sit with. I wrote this book to bring the truth into the light after decades of darkness. If anything in these pages helped you feel less alone in your own life journey, or offered even a moment of breath, recognition, or insight, I'm grateful.

As you step back into your own life, one question I return to again
and again is this:

How can I bring more joy to myself and the world today?